NATYA YO

PERFORMING & VISUAL ARTS SERIES

2

NATYA YOGA

PEACE PASSION PAIN
MAPPING EMOTIONS

ANJALI & R. SRIRAM

MOTILAL BANARSIDASS
PUBLISHING HOUSE • DELHI
Email: mlbd@mlbd.in • Website: www.mlbd.in

*First Edition : Delhi, **2023***

Illustration and Sketches by : Clemens Maurer
Author's Photo by : Irene Niessen

ISBN: 978-93-5676-042-4 (Hardcover)
ISBN: 978-93-5676-043-1 (Paperback)

Printed & Published by
Rajendra P Jain *for*
Motilal Banarsidass Publishing House
A-44, Naraina Industrial Area, Phase I,
New Delhi–110 028 (INDIA)
Email: mlbd@mlbd.in
Website: www.mlbd.in

CONTENTS

FOREWORD

The authors of this delightful and illuminating book need no introduction from me. A couple who have dedicated their lives in different disciplines with the same goal at heart: the cultivation of love and serenity as a way of life. The cultivation of serenity demands a profound understanding of human emotions.

This book brings to life the way two different disciplines – yoga and dance – shed light on our understanding of the emotions. The authors are leading lights in their separate fields, and each brings a lifetime's wisdom and study to the subject. The book presents a blend of both art forms to illuminate not only the emotions themselves and the power they embody, but how they can be harmonized in the human heart. Approaching emotions through classical texts on yoga and dance (Nāṭya), whether expressing them in the teaching space or on stage, or dealing with them in daily life – for Anjali and Sriram, the subject of emotions has been a life-long investigation.

In 1969, Anjali Sriram graduated in Performing Arts from the State School of Dramatic Arts and Music in Stuttgart and had her debut with the Staatstheater Stuttgart the same year.

In 1971 she moved to London and it was here that her love for Indian culture and lifelong passion for Bharatanatyam began. In 1974 she moved to San Francisco to perform with the Dance Theatre of Om, and in 1976 enrolled at the prestigious fine art and performance academy, Kalakshetra in Madras (Chennai). Since then, she has performed solo all over the world, introducing new audiences to the marvels of Bharatanatyam. Her passion for poetry took her into writing, and she has published several books in German, including three novels, one based on the Silappathikaram, another on women in the Bible. The entire Ramayana forms the background of her third novel based in South India and in the USA.

R. Sriram, from Chennai, has been teaching yoga since the 1980s in India and across Europe. He was a close student of T.K.V. Desikachar for over thirty years and also attended many group sessions with Desikachar's father, one of the foremost yoga teachers in the world, T. Krishnamacharya. Sriram's ability to blend Indian traditions and western pragmatism in his classes has made him a popular as well as highly respected teacher. His translation and interpretation of the *Yogasūtra of Patanjali* from Sanskrit into German highlights the relevance of this ancient text to modern-day life and has become a standard edition among the entire German-speaking yoga community. Sriram is also an expert on Vedic chanting and yoga therapy and has published several books and CDs on these topics. The couple split their time between Germany and their agroforestry and rewilding project, Base, in South India close to Kodaikanal.

John McLaughlin, Pioneer of Jazz Fusion
Founder of the East-West fusion group, Shakti

EDITOR'S NOTE

Motilal Banarsidass Publishing House (MLBD) has earned well-deserved international eminence as a highly respected publisher of scholarly works on Indology, including Asian religions, history, culture, philosophies, arts, architecture, archaeology, language, literature, linguistics, musicology, mysticism, yoga, tantra, traditional medicine, astronomy and astrology.

This *Performing and Visual Arts Series* is a significant additional focus to their remarkable contributions to Indology in all its multi-faceted aspects and I feel privileged to serve as Chief Editor of this series. Motivated by the vision of Rajendra Prakash Jain (MLBD Chairperson), I have accepted this inspiring challenge with the able support of Associate Editor, Shovana Narayan and the Editorial Panel consisting of Indumati Raman, Divya Dayal, Parwati Dutta, Prasad Bhide and Vithal Nadkarni.

MLBD publications on history, philosophy, religion and mythology were prominent in my university studies since the late 1960's, only half of the existence of this academic publishing house. As a Fulbright and later Smithsonian scholar, I have always depended upon MLBD for non-fiction treasures and look forward to adding to these with this focused series on Performing and Visual Arts. In the past, they have published fine work on Indian theatre, Rasa theory, Hindustani music and dance. This series seeks to broaden the scope and enrich the available works that cover a panorama of visual arts and architecture, multiple dance, theatre, puppetry and musical genres and their import.

Just as it is essential to look back in order to move forward, attention to living traditions will contextualize the theoretical discourse relevant to contemporary practice. We look forward to sharing a wide range of performing and visual arts thoughts, ideas, research and practice in this on-going series. As I expand my own horizons across this aesthetic landscape, I hope you will also enjoy sharing this engaging journey.

We are delighted to begin the series with *Natya Yoga - Peace Passion Pain Mapping Emotions* by Anjali & R. Sriram and *Relevance of Embellishments in the Indian Raga System* by Dr Divya Dayal.

The cultivation of serenity demands a profound understanding of human emotions. *Natya Yoga* brings to life the way two different disciplines – yoga and dance – approaching emotions through classical texts on yoga and dance (Nāṭya) aimed at the cultivation of love and serenity as a way of life. Author Anjali Sriram, trained at the State School of Dramatic Arts and Music in Stuttgart, performed at the Staatstheater, Stuttgart, with San Francisco's Dance Theatre of Om followed by advanced training at, Kalakshetra. R. Sriram has been teaching yoga since the 1980s in India and across Europe, a close student of T.K.V. Desikachar for over thirty years. His translation and interpretation of the Yogasūtra of Patanjali into German has become a standard edition among the entire German-speaking yoga community.

John McLaughlin, Guitarist and Pioneer of Jazz Fusion has written the foreword to their fascinating book.

In the foreword to *Relevance of Embellishments in the Indian Raga System* by Dr Divya Daya, Richard Widdess, Professor Emeritus of Musicology, SOAS University of writes "Divya Dayal could not have chosen a more important subject for her book than the art and craft of melodic embellishment in the classical vocal music of North India. It is difficult to go beyond classification in order to discuss the application, function and aesthetic effects of embellishment, in the contexts of performance and musical culture more generally. By analyzing specific compositions as they have been notated, exploring the relationship of embellishments to rāga-s, interviews with established gharānā representatives and younger exponents her work is both valuable in itself, and helpful in suggesting avenues for further research."

Sharon Lowen
Chief Editor,
MLBD Performing and Visual Arts Series

INTRODUCTION

For us as authors - a dancer and a yoga practitioner - it has long been our desire to bring together the aesthetics of Indian art and the philosophical thought behind yoga.

There is a common assumption that a dancer – or any artist for that matter – is attached to her or his own body, voice and dreams and tends to be vain, whereas a yogi aspires to the exact opposite. In this book we wish to do away with the preconception that a serious practitioner of yoga is a dry, emotionless being removed from reality, while an artist is temperamental and impulsive, overreacts to their surroundings and is very often in love with their own convictions. This book is also our attempt to show the union between Indian art and yoga: something we have come to appreciate in our own personal life.

Peace as contentment, fulfilment or enlightenment seems at first to be the opposite of passion, as fury, anger or rage; and also seems in no way connected to love, as attraction, desire or affection. This is not in fact, the case.

Understanding the emotions is one of the most important and most taxing of life's tasks. This book deals with a range of phenomena that fall under the umbrella term of 'emotion' – everything from seemingly permanent states of mind to fleeting feelings, from psychological states to sentiments and mental blocks.

How to deal with the emotions without getting carried away by them and how to find role models for relationships is examined through the ideas in two foundational texts: the *Yogasūtra* of Patanjali and the *Nāṭyaśāstra* of Bharatamuni.

ACKNOWLEDGEMENT

We are deeply indebted to the teachers who have guided and inspired us in developing our understanding of Yoga and Nāṭya:

Teachers from the Kalakshetra tradition, first and foremost Srimati Shanta Dhananjayan and Sri V.P. Dhananjayan, as also Srimati Uma Rao and Srimati Anandhi Ramachandran.

Dance master, V. Muthuswamy Pillai.

Yoga Masters, Sri T.K.V. Desikachar and Sri T. Krishnamacharya.

Sanskrit pandits, Sri Srinivasacharya and Sri A.S. Subbukrishna Srowthy.

We thank Priya Nagesh, Thiruvannamalai, who read the manuscript several times and gave us valuable suggestions.

We also thank Anita Roy, who did the final editing.

GUIDE TO PRONUNCIATION OF SANSKRIT WORDS

SPECIAL SYMBOLS	PRONUNCIATION
a	mug
ā	mart
i	mint
ī	meet
u	wood
ū	mood
e	mate
o	moat
ai	might
au	mouse
c	match
s	mast
ś	mache
ṣ	marsh
ñ	señor
d/t	tongue by the teeth
ḍ/ṭ	with the tip of the tongue against the palate
(ṁ)	the preceding syllable becomes nasal
(ḥ)	thc preceding vocal becomes aspirate

1

NĀṬYA AND YOGA

For thousands of years, yoga has been recognized as an invaluable way to regain or retain our vitality and health. People who practice yoga often seem to achieve a better understanding of themselves and their needs. As the popularity of yoga in the modern world increases every year, it is important to reflect on its roots and keep its context in mind. This helps to deepen our practice, so that we come to the heart of yoga and to the core of ourselves. It also helps to cast a different/clearer light on the complex inner world of the emotions.

An intense practice of yoga sensitizes body and mind, and thereby our emotionality. If such an intense practice is uprooted from its core and lacks a context supporting it, it may oversensitize us, thereby exposing the fragility of our mind and rendering us emotionally vulnerable. By understanding emotions in the originally intended context of yoga and finding means to deal with them, a serious yoga practitioner learns to avoid being uprooted or overwhelmed by feelings and passions.

The yoga texts – and above all the Yogasūtra – give

us clear steps on how to give our sadhana (practice) the foundation it needs to remain a sadhana of yoga and not just a way to improve our physical fitness.

The essence of Sāṃkhya, the ancient philosophical school which is the basis of yoga, lies in the text *Sāṃkhyakārikā*. This text repeatedly draws on analogies from the arts to bring out the relationship between reality and stage. The interplay between the actor and the spectator, or the canvas and the painting, or the actor and the director is much like the interplay between the thinker and the self that is a witness of the thinking. Awareness of this interplay gives us the space needed to understand life and its goal. This is where we came upon the idea to connect yoga, the arts of life and nāṭya, the arts of stage.

Nāṭya – drama and dance – wishes to establish peace, calmness, happiness, self-confidence and freedom for the spectator as well as for the artist. It wants to lessen sorrow and pain. Nāṭya is an important subject as it visualizes the aims of yoga. 'Play' as a concept is prevalent in the Indian systems of philosophy. Seeing life as a 'līla' or 'play' gives the lightness necessary to respect the rules of the game of life on the one hand, while keeping a distance from the surprises that life can spring on us, on the other. Tragedies as well as comedies need to be enjoyed by the Rasikas. They are a meditation on emotions and make the onlooker understand dharma (the responsibility in one's life), artha (dealing with the material world) and kāma (dealing with the desire for pleasure).

All Indian arts recreate what nature reveals. They also fine-tune the way we look at life and its happenings, the beauty (saundarya) as well as the tragedies (duhkha) around us. Appreciating the aesthetics and the sentiment of sringara – that which attracts – by observing emotions in dance and drama, the audience can get a larger view of the role of yoga. It reveals to us simultaneously the beauty in nature as well as the cruelties of reality.

In profound phases of history, wherever in the world they took place, the nourishment of the arts was given great priority and importance. Indian art, which is considered a form of yoga, is a serious spiritual pursuit – namely freeing ourselves from the intermittent thinking of the self and allowing our minds to become absorbed in a deeper reality, which we may recognize as love, beauty or creativity. To arrive at an experience of these aspects of reality, certain prime or permanent existing emotions play a crucial role. We can neither ignore them, nor let them be subsumed under the waves of other myriad emotions and subtle feelings which randomly ebb and flow. The discovery of the idea of prime emotions is a very important milestone as we learn to grapple with the entire spectrum of human emotions.

The contents of the Nāṭyaśāstra cannot be confined to the field of the performing arts alone. Their reach is far wider, and their validity universal. According to the Nāṭyaśāstra, dance, drama and music can show the path to a more fulfilled life as well as to a deep spiritual development. It is on this basis that we have taken the liberty of interpreting its contents and making extrapolations based on the way it deals with the subject of emotions.

Also, the Yogasūtras quoted in this book are not all verbatim translations of the individual sutra. The translations are very close to the original but are worded so as to make them more accessible to the modern reader.

A schism out of place

Body and mind are interlinked. Anyone practicing yoga intensely gets the experience that there is no real difference between the body and the mind. Every serious effort at understanding our body is influenced by the state of our mind and vice versa. Every deep effort at studying them disparately will bring us to a point where we have to drop the idea that the mind and the body are two distinct entities.

> *Deep meditation on strength leads to the strength of an elephant.* – *Yogasūtra 3.24*

Mind and body are different aspects of our physical being but they cannot really be separated from each other or even viewed individually. They follow each other and interact all the time. Fear affects our physical health and happiness makes us look beautiful.

Thoughts and emotions are even less disparate entities than body and mind. They mean different things at the level of language, but when it comes down to the level of experience, the distinction is blurred. If we were asked the question, 'Are they really two different things?' we may reply according to how we normally deal with these terms, and we would probably say 'Yes'. However, when we answer that very same question after we have attained a calm and meditative state of mind, the answer would be 'No'.

When we speak of loving someone, do we mean the tender thoughts we have towards this person or the gush of emotions evoked by their presence? When we hate somebody, is it the hateful thoughts that disturb us or the anger we feel towards the person? If we try to find an answer to this question, the idea of a contrariness between what is thought and what is emotion is bound to resolve. Quietening the thoughts quietens the emotions and vice versa. We will have to keep this fact in mind as we begin to look at and understand emotions and leave the schism behind.

Two qualities, dispassion and peacefulness, are a prerequisite to understanding the mind. They are on the one hand elusive, but on the other, known to us from our own experience. These qualities are known as vairāgya (dispassion) and śānta (calmness). Both are necessary for understanding and dealing with emotions. The word dispassion is synonymous with serenity, detachment and objectivity. The word peacefulness is synonymous with tranquillity, composure and calmness.

Looking and seeing are by themselves important tools in shaping the mind: looking at the self and the other. The way we look at ourselves is almost always an indication of the state of our own observing mind. The ultimate task in yoga is to grow into a dispassionate spectator of the self and a compassionate spectator of the other. Based on these yogic qualities of being dispassionate and compassionate, the masters have given us ideas to understand emotions. We learn to cultivate the role of the spectator; to be able to look outside as well as inside ourselves dispassionately, in a detached, non-judgemental way. That helps us avoid drowning in an emotion but watch it with equanimity as it continues to play with us. Reflecting on emotions when the heat of an emotion has cooled off helps us in becoming a peaceful onlooker.

> *In the absence of calmness, observation is influenced by the impressions which are already there in our mind.*
>
> – *Yogasūtra 1.4*

The Yogasūtra says that when we are dispassionate – in the sense of being able to remain the inner witness and not get swept away by the vagaries of the mind – we become masters of the emotions.

Imagine you are trekking through the jungle, quietly observing the natural world around you. You will be impressed by the grace and the beauty of plants and creatures. You feel empathy with them in their pain and understanding towards them in their fight for survival. You see that their existence does not need your involvement. That is the beginning of a detached observation which can lead to vairāgya. The basic emotions of love, compassion, conviviality and forgivingness then grow naturally in you. They arise spontaneously because they are imbedded in all of us. Whenever we have a dispassionate and neutral attitude towards the people with whom we are dealing, such dispassion will kindle the finest emotions and enhance our humane sides. It is out of such a dispassionate attitude alone that we can be non-judgemental and neutral, remain unhurried and shed fears: this can go a long way into making our efforts compassionate and meaningful. If we were full of aversion towards whoever has caused the distress we wish to alleviate, and thereby be scared, angry or hasty, the act of our compassion is bound to lack the quality it needs to alleviate the distress.

The cultivation of dispassion or vairāgya is a fundamental task in yoga to establish the quality of sattva, the balanced state of mind. In fact, the only way to tackle pain is by removing what Patanjali calls 'saṃyoga', the inability to keep an observer's distance to what we observe. Yoga practice is the playground on which we develop the skill of dispassion. Observe the breath, the body, the silence, the disturbing thoughts – all of them with dispassion, in a detached way.

In the context of emotions, it is important to remember that dispassion is not about removing or overcoming passion but is the very starting point of compassion!

Suffering ensues, when the inner Observer gets entangled with the observed object.– Yogasūtra 2.17

What does the Nāṭyaśāstra, the text on performing arts, teach us about dispassion? We read here about śānta, the quietness of mind, as a primary emotion. Śānta is the substratum of all feelings, which helps us understand, deal with and correctly portray emotions.

Śānta or peacefulness becomes the anchor when the whirlwind of other emotions tries to carry us away. The Nāṭyaśāstra speaks of nine basic, prime or permanent existing human emotions, with śānta, or calmness, as the first and most basic of them all. Love, disgust, courage, anger, amusement, fear, astonishment and compassion are the eight other prime emotions intrinsic to all human beings. We cannot consider any of them as 'bad'. However, when we are in the grip of these, we are also engulfed with many other sub-emotions like jealousy or pride. The idea is to remain aware of śānta as the base. It may motivate us towards a meaningful action.

Calmness, in conjunction with dispassion, is an invaluable key to be able to handle emotional onslaughts, whether they come from within or without. The mind needs to be without preconception, like a white screen ready to receive the colour of the emotions. The white screen is the base to look at all these eight emotions. This is why we begin the book with śānta and vairāgya. Imagine a disturbed, hysterical mind entering a lonely house, getting into a fit of fear and maybe even fainting. Now imagine a calm mind entering a lonely house: it will experience fear as something which makes it cautious and observant. Shanta invokes the quality of sattva, the balanced state.

Whose
body is the universe,
speech is in every sound
ornaments are the moon and the stars,
to that Sattva, Śiva I bow!

– *Abhinayadarpanam 1*

Patanjali and Bharatamuni are two masterminds. Patanjali is India's divine scientist from an early millennium. He delved deep into the heart, mind and soul of the human being, developed the art of yoga and presented it to mankind as the Sanskrit text we know as the Yogasūtra. Given its antiquity, we do not know the original date of the work, the versions which are the basis for the modern editions date back to the 3rd century. Patanjali is surely among the shining beacons of the ancient world whose profound script offers wisdom of the highest level and whose pertinence needs to be discovered in today's world.

Bharatamuni was a sage and master who blended arts, the human mind, stage and philosophy into his work, which is dated around 200 BCE. His work seems to be based on the theatre and dance forms existing at that time, as well as on a deep understanding of the human mind and relationships. It is improbable that there ever was or is, a body of work, which so beautifully intertwines the subjects of performing arts, aesthetics, philosophy, spirituality and the human mind as the Nāṭyaśāstra. The versions which are the basis for the modern editions date back to the 7th century.

In the initial verses of the Nāṭyaśāstra, Bharatamuni explains the origin of Nāṭya: long, long ago people of this world goaded by greed, jealousy and anger took to vulgar ways of life. The gods approached the Creator, Brahma, and requested him to give something which would not only be educative but also pleasing both to the eyes and the ears. Brahma went into meditation and composed the Nāṭyaveda. He gave it to the gods, declaring that it shall be practised by beings who are clever, intelligent, observant and self-controlled.

The way the Nāṭyaśāstra looks at emotions handled on stage becomes a path for handling relationships and achieving the goals of life. Bharatamuni's work evokes Shakespeare's famous image that all the world's a stage, and men and women merely players on it.

The goal of Yoga is straightforward, it is the art of being at home in oneself. Take on a task which is appealing to you and turn your mind inward: keep at it relentlessly, rest assured that guidance will come. Trust the power of your efforts and try not to anticipate results. Practice your personal way of yoga, resting in the awareness of the cosmic force that envelopes and supports you. Let your practice integrate every aspect of your system – relationships, body, breath, senses and mind. This will give a meditative quality to your day-to-day life, make you conscious of the unchanging eye ('I') within you, and enable a sharp perception of the outer world rather than one blurred by the ever-changing flux of the individual ego.

Art is yoga showing that the drama of an individual life is very similar to what we call nature, the macrocosm or prakṛti. This is consistent with the fundamental belief in the

Vedic texts that the human being echoes, at the microcosmic level, the macrocosm of the universe. The aesthetics of Bharatamuni's Nāṭyaśāstra is exemplified in its presentation of the close intertwining of life and stage; nature and art; the philosophy of life and the psychology of an individual. On the one hand, it portrays an art form. On the other, the scripture also delves into philosophy and spirituality, revealing an incredibly profound understanding of the human mind, making the art of Nāṭya one of the preeminent pathways to the goal of yoga.

Sensory perception, reasoning and adaptive learning from the environment are three tools that even the tiniest creatures use in order to change and evolve. Human beings, however, have the faculty to perceive reality directly, in a very deep way which transcends the senses and is free of the subjective bias of the individual. When this deep, non-personalized perception, free of opinion and personal goals, evolves, a fundamental change can take place in us and revolutionize our being. The art of yoga and yoga in arts aim at developing this capacity for deep perception that can enable this change in us.

Knowledge is acquired through direct perception,
inference and reliable sources. – *Yogasūtra 1.6*

Nāṭya as a yogic realisation gives even greater bliss than meditating on the supreme being. Great sages like Nārada were captivated by Nāṭya, therefore Nāṭyaśāstra is considered to be the fifth Veda.

2

ŚĀNTA AND VAIRĀGYA

Calmness and Detachment

Śānta, a calm state of mind, is the basis of all creativity. It is the first step of any artistic endeavour – rising above personal involvement and aiming at a universal approach to things. To arrive at a state of śānta and be able to reflect without adding personal colour to things, remains an important quest for any spiritual seeker.

Vairāgya, the state where the mind is aware of the impermanence of worldly matters and remains aloof to them, is key to reaching a state of śānta. It helps to observe without being judgmental and to understand dispassionately. How to attain such consciousness is a fundamental question for anyone starting on the path of yoga.

Indian mythology helps to grasp śānta through Nārāyana, the image of the eternal, reclining on the coils of the divine snake Adiśeṣa on the surface of the infinite ocean. Adiśeṣa lies curled on the milky ocean with his hood raised – balanced, watchful and quiet. Nārāyana reclines on this stable and soft bed, his head raised, silently listening to what is happening in the universe. This mythological picture of Nārāyana is also an artistic representation of the state of mind called śānta.

The Nāṭyaśāstra describes śānta as the first emotion, white in colour. It is a state in which the mind is like a white screen capable of reflecting the colours of all the emotions. Here we are in touch with the 'seer' within us, the true 'eye' behind our senses, which receives dispassionately all our impressions of the world.

> *If our illusions end, our expectations end too and*
> *the inner Observer stays disentangled from the*
> *observed object.* – *Yogasūtra 2.25*

The road to developing vairāgya or detachment lies in the awareness of two inherent layers of the self: the non-personal self, the 'seer' and the ever-changing personal self. On one hand is the unchanging, permanently alert self and on the other, the self which is constantly reacting to and involved with what is going on around us. Becoming conscious of the discretely different roles of the two sides of 'ourselves' is a way to establish calmness. In this way, one can cultivate the dispassionate attitude that we need in daily life to retain an attitude of peace in the midst of turmoil all around.

Sāṃkhyakārikā uses a metaphor to describe the relationship between the two layers of our self, between the non-personal permanent self and the ever-changing personal self, which revolves around it. The two are likened to the spectator and the performer, the permanent and the changing self, respectively. The dancer continues with the performance, while the spectator keeps watching. This continues based on the mutually dependent fulfilment each is seeking: wanting 'it' to be seen and wanting to see 'it'. This attraction between their roles grows. The climax of this mutual attraction comes when the spectator, being fulfilled by the essence behind the dance, exclaims, "I have seen the essence of the dance!" while the dancer, realizing that the essence of the dance has been recognized, exclaims, "The essence of the dance has been seen!" This is the moment where both spectator and dancer attain freedom from the yearning to see and to be seen.

This can be interpreted as the instance when the onlooker within us, the seer, sees the drama which our emotions perform. One could also look at it as the instance when the dance of the mind attains such a refinement that the onlooker within recognizes it in its entirety. It is the yogic state of mind where the mind has attained such a state of calmness, that it is reflected in the deep non-personal self within. The dancer symbolizes 'prakṛti' or 'citta' (the personal self), and the spectator symbolizes 'puruṣa' or 'draṣṭā' (the non-personal seer).

Something similar can happen between the dancer and the spectator in an actual performance of nāṭya.

The quality of śānta enables the performer entering the stage to mirror all emotions through gestures and expressions during the performance. By staying detached, the attitude of spectatorship is integrated into her or his own performance. The onlooker links into the peaceful state of śānta state of the performer and benefits directly from it. The onlooker can enjoy all the emotions together with the performer, irrespective of whether these emotions are happy or woeful. This common experience of spectator and performer is called rasa, which literally means taste.

In the role of a peaceful spectator of an imaginary situation, one can watch the core of the emotion dispassionately without engaging with the web of personal emotional impressions around it and getting drawn in or caught up in it. Even though one is confronted by the emotions, one can look at them, enjoy their essence, and thereby get knowledge of their true nature.

Rasa in Indian aesthetics is a unique philosophical approach to explore the essence of feelings and experience them in a detached way. Rasa is both taste and also the enjoyment given by the taste. It is through rasa that not only the performing stage, but also the world around, begins to present itself as a stage. In the Vedas, the Eternal Being itself is equated to rasa. The divine manifests itself in a rasa-experience.

raso vai saḥ – *Taittirīya Upaniṣat 2.7*

By cultivating the rasa-experience not only nāṭya, but life itself can be regarded as a play. One can learn to be a spectator of what is happening all around, and to cultivate a dispassionate and non-judgemental attitude, wherein one remains level-headed and in a state of equanimity. This is a road to attaining vairāgya. The personal self and the surrounding world are then like a spectacle on a stage which one observes from the level of a deep impersonal self. In this way we begin to see the world as a līla or a cosmic play in which we have a role. (It is true of course, these roles come with tasks that need to be fulfilled. We shall come to this in a later chapter.)

Only when the performer's portrayal has a depth based in śānta, can rasa be tasted. Otherwise, not only would the performer be carried away by the emotions, it may also lead to the spectator getting carried away by them. Catharsis, the experience of an ecstatic climax resulting from identification and involvement, is valid in the tradition of Greek theatre, not in the Indian. The effect of a cleansing through emotion is contrary to the concept of rasa. Catharsis drives towards an ecstatic experience, while Indian theatre aims at a reflective experience.

During the rasa-experience an inner bell rings in the spectator, who then remembers the portrayed emotion from their own past experience. There is the awareness that 'I am the spectator' and therefore detached from the happenings on stage. Therefore, nāṭya is not only an entertainment but a meditation too. While watching the emotional states presented by the artist on the stage, on canvas or in books, the spectator or reader unconsciously remembers his or her past personal experience of the emotion and reflects upon them in the present.

Śānta as well as vairāgya enhance the mood for meditation. The dancer who is in the state of śānta will be able to mirror emotions and the spectator can enjoy them and experience rasa or essence in a meditative way. The empathy of the yogi in the state of vairāgya will reveal their detachment and inspire others. The concept of vairāgya in yoga, the science of the spirit, is close to the concept of śānta in nāṭya and its theory of aesthetics.

> *In the state of yoga, the deepest core of our self,*
> *the 'inner Seer', remains untouched by the impression,*
> *sees the things as they are, and – like a white screen –*
> *becomes a mirror for the deepest reflection.*
>
> *– Yogasūtra 4.22*

Nāṭyaśāstra speaks of eight sentiments or permanent emotions, which have as their base the ninth, śānta, and are

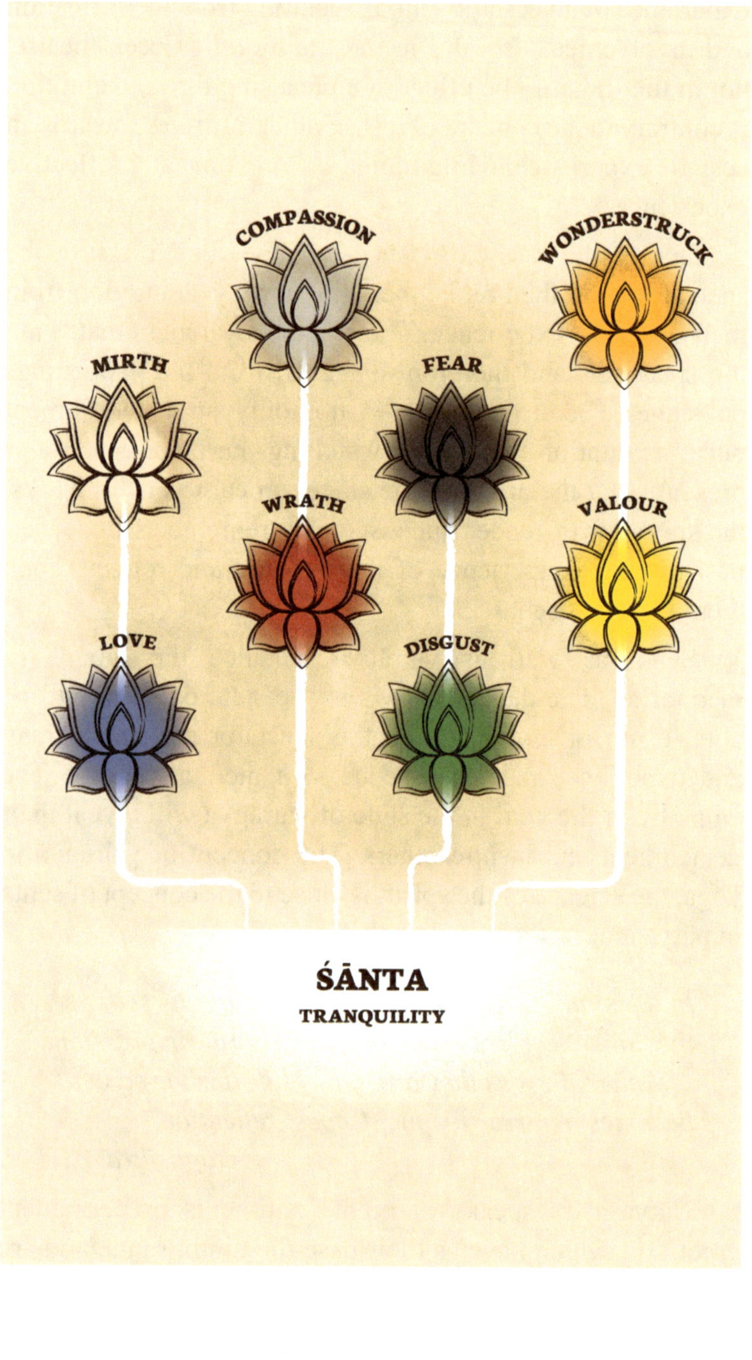
COMPASSION
WONDERSTRUCK
MIRTH
FEAR
WRATH
VALOUR
LOVE
DISGUST
ŚĀNTA
TRANQUILITY

each linked to one of the eight rasas. These eight are love, courage, anger, disgust, courage, amusement, compassion, astonishment and fear.

> *The source Rasas are four: Śṛṅgāra - erotic, Vīra - heroic, Raudra - terror and Bībhatsa - disgust.*
> *Hāsya, humour results when love is imitated,*
> *a terrible thing or situation produces Kāruṇya, pity,*
> *a heroic deed appears Adbhuta, marvellous and*
> *anything disgusting produces Bhayānaka, fright.*
> *– Nāṭyaśāstra VI. 39-45*

A person in the state of śānta will be able to enjoy the eight rasas, the emotional experiences, with the detachment of an onlooker. When other feelings like jealousy, grief or excitement arise, they will be seen as fleeting or non-permanent feelings which merely support and heighten the eight permanent emotions. They will surface like waves over a peaceful sea, rising and falling. A person attuned to the state of śānta will not get drowned by them, but regard them as fleeting, transitory emotions and impressions, which will ebb away.

Śānta is the centre of meditation. If we develop śānta, we can concentrate our minds and focus our senses. Our compassion is awakened, and the capacity for abstract thinking and understanding complex subjects develops.

> *In a one-pointed mind,*
> *the constant focus will be a steady surface,*
> *on which impressions will rise and ebb away.*
> *– Yogasūtra 3.12*

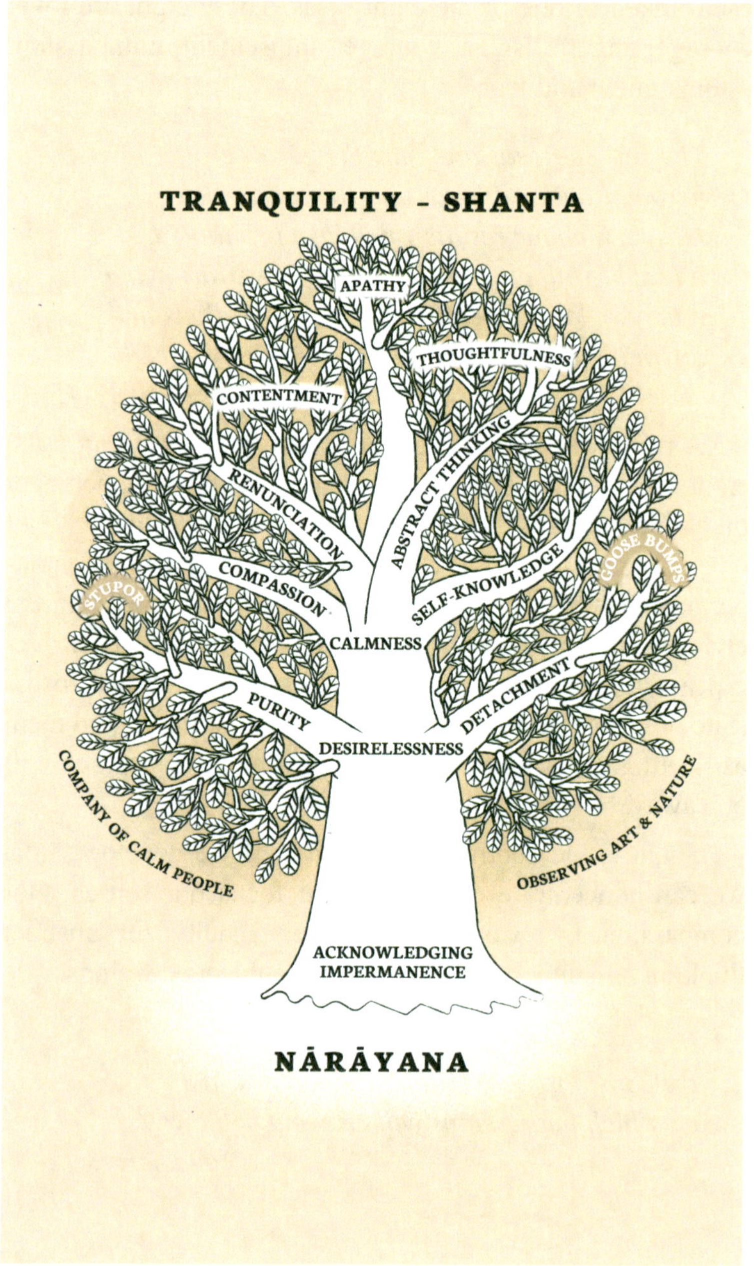
TRANQUILITY - SHANTA
APATHY
THOUGHTFULNESS
CONTENTMENT
RENUNCIATION
ABSTRACT THINKING
COMPASSION
SELF-KNOWLEDGE
GOOSE BUMPS
STUPOR
CALMNESS
PURITY
DETACHMENT
DESIRELESSNESS
COMPANY OF CALM PEOPLE
OBSERVING ART & NATURE
ACKNOWLEDGING IMPERMANENCE
NĀRĀYANA

Inspirations from a great master of our times

T. Krishnamacharya definitely is one of the most valuable sources of Yoga in the 20th century. He was the teacher of the three world renowned masters B.K.S. Iyengar, Pattabhi Jois and T. K. V. Desikachar. He was versatile in the texts of Yoga, Vedanta, Vishistha-Advaita, Sanskrit and Ayurveda, as well as ancient arts and poetry. Inspite of his orthodox background and inspite of his being submersed in the world of the ancient texts, he was universal in his thinking and had the phenomenal capacity of blending all his knowledge and adapting them to the current times in which we are living. In *Mokṣa Mārga*, Alamelu Seshadri and T.K. Sribhashyam write on this subject as they learnt it from their father, Sri T. Krishnamacharya, who, they write, drew on the classical epics, Ramayana and Śrīmad Bhāgavatam, the Upanishads as well as the commentary of Vedanta Desikar on the Sudarśanacakra. Krishnamacharya says:

Śānta is the natural condition of our deep inner self. It is based on an innate disposition towards liberation and the absence of desire. Human beings are born with śānta and gradually develop the other basic eight emotions. The eight petals of emotions issue from the flower of serenity. Human beings are blessed simultaneously with detachment as well as with the will to love and enjoy the world of experience. Śānta is our sthāyi bhāva, our main and prime emotion. While it is there for us to remain unruffled and calm towards and in the world, the other eight help us to live in and with the world. As children we are in a state of balance. However, we become caught in the web of desire and greed, thereby losing the link to underlying śānta.

Some of the basic emotions move in correspondingly opposing directions: When the feeling of disgust grows, we lose astonishment; when fear increases, we lose courage; when anger increases, we lose compassion; when the feeling of disgust grows, we lose love. But when we lose love, we also lose peace. Maintaining śānta and śṛṅgāra, calmness and love, will not only protect us from the domination of the other seven emotions, but also from being led away by all the auxiliary, fleeting emotions.

> *"We conquer disdain by love, violence by compassion, fear by courage and repulsion by wonder. All the four lead us to peace, serenity and calmness." – Way to Liberation: Mokṣa Mārga, T. Krishnamacharya's teachings through his daughter and son, Alamelu Sheshadri and T.K. Sribhashyam*

Ideas to develop śānta

According to the Nāṭyaśāstra too, love or śṛṅgāra is the first emotion which grows. To protect and nurture śānta is possible only by developing the emotion of śṛṅgāra, love. In life, love alone can help maintain śānta.

Śānta is associated with the colour white, and the deity, Nārāyaṇa.

Here we present some ideas, derived from the Nāṭyaśāstra, which can help to develop or cultivate śānta:

- Śānta can be developed by observing nature, training in the arts or practising yoga holistically.
- Śānta grows when we recognize the impermanence of life and the world and reflect upon it.
- We get inspired into śānta by meeting with wise and learned people and saints.

Yoga too gives us a comprehensive set of practices which together help to find to inner peace and clarity. The eight-parted practice of yoga is what is called Aṣṭāṅgayoga.

A comprehensive practice of yoga comprises eight parts: disciplines involving

1) *the way we deal with other beings,*
2) *the way we conduct our daily life,*
3) *our physical posture,*
4) *our knowledge of the breath*
5) *our awareness of our senses; as well as*
6) *concentrating our mind on a meditative topic,*
7) *keeping up the concentration with a deep quietness of mind and*
8) *learning to let go of all the mental clutches we hold on to.*

– *Yogasūtra 2.29*

3

BHĀVANĀ

Four Emotions for Meditation

Yoga is the state in which all mental activities
(which include thoughts and emotions) flow evenly.
In the state of yoga, the inner 'seer'
becomes apparent to us. – *Yogasūtra 1.2 & 1.3*

The word *bhāva* comes from the root *bhu* which means 'to be' or 'to become'. It means that from an emotional perspective we become that which we imagine or visualize to be. Bhāva is the outward expression of what is happening within us. When our thoughts and emotions focus on beauty, a smile may appear on our face. This smile is the bhāva of beauty. When observation, visualization and concentration come together, they create an emotional effect which we call a bhāva. Bhāvas can become deep states of experience, which then express themselves through our actions and attitudes, both in body and in mind.

The Yogasūtra talks about four particular emotional states: the bhāvanās. Bhāvanās are bhāvas which are conducive for deep reflection and meditation. They are patterns of emotional reactions which are true to our unsullied nature. With these four bhāvanās the mind can become quiet, like a reflecting surface. Therefore, the four bhāvanās that are encouraged in the Yogasūtra as tools to experience meditation are: maitrī (friendliness), karuṇā (compassion), muditā (enthusiasm) and upeksā (forgiveness).

These four emotions are imbedded in us: we need not seek them out. They arise spontaneously in situations where we are neutral and open. Friendliness, compassion, enthusiasm or forgiveness are four emotions which are ever ready to flower within us, if the situation calls for it and our minds are open. For example, when we see an innocent child, it evokes love and friendliness in us. If we see the child lose its balance, fall and hurt herself, it prompts us to act quickly with spontaneous compassion. When we see her overcome her limitations and attain a new skill, we become enthusiastic and encourage her. On seeing the child misbehave, we try to understand the circumstances and be forgiving towards the child. These reactions are natural tendencies of all human beings. They are all inherent in us. The beauty in the child's innocence evokes our love, her grief moves us to compassion, her learning of skills makes us enthusiastic and we show understanding for her misbehaviour while being aware of potential problems.

Cultivating and understanding the Bhāvanās

When we visualize how it is to be compassionate, we become aware that compassion already exists within us. When we see a compassionate person, we are not only moved by her or his feelings, we also see that the compassion within us is awakened. Similarly seeing a person drawn to beauty draws out the friendliness in us. The same holds good for all the bhāvanās. By focussing on them or associating ourselves with them, we will find a natural way of growing into and expressing these emotions – friendliness, compassion, enthusiasm and forgiveness.

But imagine it is not an innocent child in front of us, but a person towards whom we nurture negative feelings. This person's innocence may fill us with envy, his pain may create hatred in us, his successes, cynicism and his misbehaviour, righteousness. Our emotional reactions are very much based on our judgements. However, by cultivating these four bhāvanās, we train our mental activities to flow evenly, bringing greater consistency to our emotional behaviour.

Through being friendly towards people who are fulfilled,
compassionate towards those who suffer,
encouraging towards those who are doing things well
and forgiving towards those who make mistakes,
our mind achieves steadiness. – *Yogasūtra 1.33*

Maitrī – friendliness and love

Attraction is rooted in us like a natural impulse that comes alive when we see beauty, innocence, creativity or happiness. It appears when we see innocent beings, or look at the perfection of nature. It is there in the love with which we approach another human being without prejudices or expectations, carrying friendliness. It subdues fleeting emotions like jealousy, pride, greed and frustration. We become happy when we come under its sway and come closer to the grace within us. Opening our eyes to innocence and beauty around us is the way to develop maitrī bhāvanā.

Karuṇā – concerned sorrow and compassion

Not to stay indifferent to the suffering of others, but to respond to it spontaneously without considering one's own needs or opinions is the ideal of compassion. If we have a profound understanding of suffering, we see the pain of the others and develop compassion for them. In the suffering of the other person, we see the suffering that is part of the whole world. A deep experience of suffering and sorrow is the basis of compassion. Only such an understanding of suffering can lead to the growth of compassion. Compassion is an emotion which is etched permanently in us. It is not a transitory emotion like despair, apathy, anxiety or weariness. It does not spring from self-negation, but from sympathizing with the suffering of the other person. It gives us the strength to refrain from seeing ourselves as the victim of suffering that is around us and to reach out compassionately to the suffering of the others.

Muditā – courage and enthusiasm

The sight of the great deeds of others provokes our enthusiasm. When we meet a person who is courageous and outspoken, it not only awakens our enthusiasm for this person, but also helps us to develop our own courage. When we are with a person who takes initiatives in the face of a hindrance and works to remove it, we are also motivated. We can discipline our mind to focus on the praiseworthy deeds of others by accepting our dependency in this world as well as focussing on the possibilities before us. In this way, we can shun sarcastic and pessimistic tendencies within us and learn to look at the positive forces, deeds and achievements around us. This will help cultivate enthusiasm and courage.

Upekṣā – being forgiving, but aware

Observing the problematic actions of other people without making righteous judgements about them, retaining one's poise by mentally maintaining a distance from them, remaining non-judgemental to enable an unbiased view of the problematic actions – this is how the emotional attitude of being forgiving and watchful at the same time can be developed. It helps us distance ourselves from undesirable things even if we are obliged to understand them, without having to run away from them or shut them out. (The word 'upekṣā' is a blend of the word roots 'upa' and 'ikṣā' which together give the meaning seeing from a distance.) The upekṣā attitude prevents us from reacting aggressively or prematurely to an incidence of aggression. It is the emotional state of every saintly person. It requires us to remain calm in order to avoid being influenced by the negative tendencies of others. We can develop this attitude by not falling prey to transitory feelings such as anger, depression, pride and self-righteousness. We discipline ourselves not to get drawn into a comparison where we give ourselves a righteous position and judge an opponent. The ability to maintain one's distance from an obviously non-righteous person who is causing pain to someone else, accrues from the commitment to compassion towards the afflicted person.

Precautions in understanding the bhāvanās

In developing the bhāvanās within ourselves, we ought not to lose sight of the essential emotions linked to them. The growth of a healthy emotion is only possible alongside some growth of mental clarity too.

- In the name of being friendly or full of love, we cannot afford to impose ourselves on the person or object to which we are strongly attracted.
- If we pity other human beings and come forward to help them with an eye on the benefits we will accrue, we will not be led into compassion.
- We cannot afford to follow an idea or a person blindly, merely because we are convinced of what he is doing and want to encourage it.
- It is not helpful to condemn things or feel superior and exclusive when we distance ourselves from things even if we are sure that they are deeply wrong. However, we have every right to express our minds clearly in a non-judgemental way.

Simple methods to cultivate bhāvanās in our daily life

Bhāvanās can be cultivated by meditation as well as through our daily activities. For example, when we grow a garden:

We choose a plant with love before we plant it (maitrī).

We remove weeds with compassion (karuṇā) for the growing plant.

We watch its growth and look after its needs carefully with enthusiasm (muditā).

We remain patient and understanding (upekṣā), as the plant bears flowers and fruits in its own time.

Activities like cooking, gardening, building houses, maintaining homes or creating art need these bhāvanās if they are to be done well. These activities will then acquire a meditative quality and enhance the growth of the bhāvanās.

If we love the activity we do, the bhāvanās are established almost automatically! Conversely, developing the bhāvanās will lead to a positive and loving environment.

Bhāvanās can also be cultivated in our day-to-day interaction with others:

Maitrī – Never become sarcastic or jealous when you encounter beauty, innocence or happiness. Be open and friendly.

Karuṇā – Learn to be compassionate, or you may become depressed and discouraged at the sight of unhappiness.

Muditā – Be enthusiastic towards others so that you can avoid becoming envious or cynical when you see great qualities in them.

Upekṣā - Never lose your neutrality, or you might turn out to be judgemental, become aggressive and even violent.

The natural world around us can also inspire us to experience bhāvanās:

When bees and butterflies gather around flowers, it reminds us of maitrī bhāvanā.

When flowers open in spring and we feel the force behind them, we are reminded of muditā bhāvanā. When a cow looks at its calf, we can feel the karuṇā bhāvanā. A tree in a storm which is firm in its roots, can inspire us to develop resilience, like in upekṣā bhāvanā.

People who have understood and imbibed bhāvanās exude love, courage, kindness and understanding. By giving it to others they lose nothing and only strengthen it in themselves. We are inspired on seeing and interacting with such persons.

Bhāvanās will obviously only develop if we reflect continually on them. By reflecting on our behaviour and reaction patterns, we can enhance them. We do not need to cultivate them in the sense of implanting these behaviour patterns into ourselves. We merely need to weed out the patterns of behaviour which really do not belong to the core of our humanity.

Bhāvanās help meditation

When the body, the senses and the mind move together, there is no distraction. We are then in a state like the current of a river as it flows in one direction with all objects floating on it, carried on its journey to the ocean. In the state of a bhāvanā, all thoughts, imagination, ideas, etc. flow in one direction and all the transitory feelings get drawn into the powerful flow of the one deep-rooted emotion from which they have emerged. In this way the bhāvanās build a solid basis for meditation.

A quietened mind is the basis for meditation. The mind becomes quiet only when the urgency and intensity behind disturbing thoughts diminish. This cannot be made to happen by suppressing thoughts. The impact of these thoughts can only be quietened through the strength of these basic emotions.

The bhāvanās are emotions which are essential to us; they are the product of a deep state of being. They help us to have dispassion towards things which are not a deep part of us, namely the transitory feelings such as jealousy, grief, being hurt etc. They open us to a new way of understanding that what Nāṭyaśāstra calls the sthāyi bhāva, or prime emotion.

Bhāvanās can help solve problems

As individuals we have inclinations and preferences. We all have one or two bhāvanās towards which we are instinctively drawn. Some people are by nature friendly and react instinctively to beauty and happiness around them whereas some others are sensitive to all suffering around them and react spontaneously with compassion. Some take immediate note of whatever praiseworthy and grand things happen around them and fall readily into an enthusiastic mood; others react in a poised way and adopt a forgiving attitude to the wrong deeds of others, without however, becoming indifferent to those wrongdoings.

Whenever we face conflict or emotional turmoil, it is important for us to take recourse to that bhāvanā which comes naturally to us. This will help steady the mind and bring out the natural equanimity within us. It will also defuse tensions in the minds of the people around us and preempt an escalation of emotionality.

> *Focus meditatively on a subject*
> *to which you have a strong inclination,*
> *that will help calm the mind.*
>
> – *Yogasūtra 1.39*

Just knowing about the bhāvanās is not going to offer a solution to problems. Thinking about them will not lead to the emotion that can motivate us. However, reflecting on them will help us become calm and to understand the different aspects of the problems around us. This will nurture the growth of the bhāvanās as well as lead us to finding suitable solutions for these problems.

Handling serious conflicts

In the event of a serious conflict, reflecting on it using all four bhāvanās can be helpful. That means each time we approach the conflict with a different state of mind, trying to understand it from different perspectives. Viewing the situation from different angles helps develop the equanimity we will need to deal with a serious conflict.

If you have doubts concerning a situation,
take a look at it from different perspectives
– *Yogasūtra 2.33*

Looking at a problem from the angle of all the bhāvanās maybe easier said than done. So let us take an example: A friend who has been reliable lets us down in a conflict situation. We could approach this situation with the following lines of thoughts, based each on the four bhāvanās:

Maitrī bhāvanā: We develop a negative picture of the friend and begin to lose faith in the idea of friendship. "Friendliness and love are not fixed upon one individual or a few individuals but are an all-embracing attitude. Otherwise, it is a mere attachment. If conviviality becomes a strong attitude in me, it will not only help win new friends, but also strengthen old friendships."

Karuṇā bhāvanā: We are shocked that the friend is insensitive to our pain and by their unwillingness to share it with us. "The world is ever-changing and suffering is always around the corner, in some form or the other. I can hardly know what suffering others are going through. My compassion is the most powerful answer to my friend's lack of understanding."

Muditā bhāvanā: We begin to smart under the feeling that, having let us down, the friend now has the upper hand. "If my mind is not centred around itself, then I do not have much to lose. A look at the larger picture will not only inspire me to be courageous, it will also help me become outspoken and bold. That will stop me from feeling like I have been used."

Upekṣā bhāvanā: We are angry, feel righteous, wish subconsciously to retaliate but overtly to leave the friendship behind. "Building opinions and coming to conclusions is not going to help the situation. I shall remain watchful but not indifferent. I shall most definitely not get drawn into any form of retaliation thereby repeating the pattern of behaviour of which I disapprove."

Reflecting on a problematic situation from all these angles can help us take a closer look at the problem, develop a distance from it and perhaps even find a solution.

Reflections

Our senses are drawn very easily to fleeting things and our mind pays a lot of attention to the transitory emotions – not only in us but also in other human beings. We need to remind ourselves constantly to keep our minds on the fundamentals.

It is invaluable for us to develop the experience of bhāvanās. In the state of bhāvanās the activities of the mind become quiet and the voice of the inner seer may be clearly heard.

The emotions corresponding to the four bhāvanās already exist in us: we merely have to become aware of them. We develop bhāvanās by observing nature and human beings who exude this state.

By meditating upon the bhāvanās,
we can strengthen the bhāvanās in us.

– Yogasūtra 3.23

4

RASA

The Taste of Emotions

The thinking mind is like the banks of a river, with emotions flowing between them like mighty currents.

What we call the mind is evident in thoughts as well as emotions. The thinking aspect of the mind is that which helps consider and weigh a situation, whereas the emotive part of the mind is that which motivates us into action and movement. Thoughts may lead to understanding, but it is emotions that help to go beyond the limits described by thought-based understanding.

Is what I am feeling true? Am I misled or manipulated by feelings of others or my own illusions? Is what I am seeing the only true reality? Such questions which arise from the core of the self cannot be answered by a thoughtful mind. A calm mind which is not overloaded by the surge of thoughts and is in a state of emotional balance alone can help to find answers. It is as though a voice deep within our hearts is whispering that our perception of reality is limited, and pushes us to look further or find out what is real and what is beyond the obvious. This pushing happens through the motivating force of deep emotions. When we become aware of the emotions which are intrinsic to and permanently lodged in us, they become bhāvas, and - like the bhāvanās - widen our perception. When we become attentive, we can savour these bhāvas, and by reflecting on them we are drawn into a mood that connects us to a greater reality.

Where the hand goes,
the eyes follow,
where the eyes are
the mind shall go;
where the mind dwells,
bhāva appears,
and where there is bhāva rasa arises.
– Abhinaya Darpaṇa, Verse 37

Based on this statement from the Nāṭya classic we could say: "Wherever the body carries us, the five senses follow and where the senses go, the mind follows and the bhāva establishes itself, giving rise to rasa."

Alternately we could say: "Concentrated action, where the mind is not scattered and there is awareness of what one is doing, creates bhava, giving rise to rasa in the world."

There are eight sthāyi bhāvas, prime or permanent emotions, which are elementary emotional forces in the universe. They play a deep-seated role within us. They may be temporarily inactive, or not easily noticed on the surface, but they are never absent. They are rooted in our subconscious and do not depend on our personal experiences to exist in us. They reveal themselves clearly when we observe them with a calm and detached mind. These eight emotions have an essential role in our life because they are the motor with which we can fuel the three main goals of our existence: dharma, artha and kāma.

> *Love, amusement, compassion, anger, courage, fear, disgust and amazement are the eight rasas.*
> – *Nāṭyaśāstra 6.15*

> *Enjoyment, amusement, sorrow, anger, enthusiasm, fear, repulsion and astonishment are proclaimed as the sthāyi bhāvas.* – *Nāṭyaśāstra 6.17*

These rasas are similar to, indeed almost the same as, the sthāyi bhāvas. Rasa is an experience between an onlooker and a performer, whilst bhāva is closely linked to an emotional state in which anyone can be.

The essential emotions of the Nāṭyaśāstra can be seen in connection with the bhāvanās of the Yogasūtra.

Śṛṅgāra: love, erotic sentiment, wanting to enjoy the object of desire

LOVE,
EROTIC SENTIMENT

In worldly life, one recognizes this sthāyi bhāva when two people are attracted to each other. Opposites attract: man attracts woman or the manliness attracts one feeling feminine and vice versa, the positive and the negative in the universe attract each other. The attraction brings out the energy of love and motivates to overcome duality. Beauty (saundarya) is one of the main factors stimulating attraction. It arouses the desire to unite. But deep behind this emotion is the pull one feels towards the ultimate spiritual union itself. This eventually leads into śānta.

Yoga philosophy speaks of a deep state of friendliness towards all beings called maitrī bhāvanā. To establish it is one of the practices in Yoga. In Nāṭya one sees this bhāva in the melting together of two people who have become one in a moment of enjoyment, when love is fulfilled and has reached its goal. Then the ultimate friendliness is established. For a person on a yogic path, it shows itself when the two opposites of the eternal divine and the mortal human – the puruṣa and the prakṛti – meet.

Vīra: courage, valour, heroism

This sthāyi bhāva shows itself readily in people who have strong willpower. Valour in everyday life is the enthusiasm with which we like to get things done or overcome hurdles. It defines that part of our personality in which we take pride. It aims at mastering things in the best possible way. This emotion reveals to us the tasks that lie ahead of us, the goals which give meaning to our life.

COURAGE, VALOUR, HEROISM

Vīra, or courage, is close to the yogic term, muditā bhāvanā, a state in which the mind is enthusiastic, positive and ready to act.

Raudra: anger, fury, rage

This will arise when there is enragement about injustice. In daily life anger is a personal reaction to something which one finds deeply unjust. Anger or wrath is a deep emotional force which surfaces as a reaction towards things which we perceive as incorrect or destructive. It wakes us up so that we protect ourselves and our surrounding from destructive and unwholesome happenings. True anger awakens our passion for and intensity towards tackling disturbing forces. Anger can be seen as a motivation to overcome indulgence and inertia. Ideally, it is a positive force that helps establish dharma or justice.

ANGER, FURY, RAGE

There is no equivalent bhāva in yoga for this, but anger can make place for understanding and compassion. Siva is a symbol of fury and terror, when he is confronted with ignorance, but as the name Siva – derived from the word for calmness – suggests, he is also the compassionate protector of all beings.

Bībhatsa: disgust, horror

This bhāva establishes itself when there is confrontation with things which are repulsive. All that is rotting and decaying or has a foul smell invokes disgust. In daily life it makes us steadfastly turn away from things we do not approve of. It helps avoiding dependencies and can lead towards vairāgya. Disgust as an emotion kindles the feeling of shame, and inhibits us from developing closeness or attachment to the things we find disgusting. It does not merely reveal the external things towards which we feel a revulsion. It can also reveal those aspects of our own life which we basically do not want to be associated with, things that distract us and lead us away from our wellbeing and chosen path.

DISGUST, HORROR

In yoga, stepping back and distancing oneself from unwanted things is called upekṣā bhāvanā. It is a process of being alert and pulling away calmly from unwholesome situations without being judgemental.

Hāsya: amusement, humour, mirth

When a situation runs contrary to the normal state of things, the sthāyi bhāva of amusement is evoked. The sight of things which are hilariously out of place leads to humour and lightheartedness. Hāsya moves us to take different and unaccustomed views of things, so that we see the world and life as a play. It reminds us that not everything is necessarily the way it appears to be; that, in retrospect, one can be amused by one's own certainties. It helps us to become lighter in attitude and not get too deeply entrenched in situations. The emotion of love helps the development of hāsya.

AMUSEMENT, HUMOUR, MIRTH

Here too, there is no corresponding bhāva in yoga. But humour helps us to remain detached from one's own stern attitudes and learn that lightness is essential for developing vairāgya. Krishna the teacher of the yoga of the Bhagavadgītā, is also the cowherd in love with all the gopīs, who are also all in love with him. In his dance, the two hands are each clasping a gopī, he multiplies his form and is repeatedly there between every two gopīs. Together they form the circle of life. His love-game is not only out of the ordinary, it is a reminder of the play in which ultimately, we are all just actors! This metaphor helps to see the closeness of the divine in our mundane lives, a thought which is valuable on the yogic path.

Kāruṇya: compassion, sorrow, pity

When there is loss of a dear one, the sthāyi bhāva of sorrow is invoked. Any tragic happening will give rise to compassion. Any deeply felt sorrow will create empathy. True compassion is always in connection with the perception of sorrow, and the urge to mitigate it. It is only by staying in touch with the sorrow that afflicts all living beings, and not merely that experienced in one's personal life, that we can differentiate between self-pitying and compassionate action.

Sorrow can arise from encountering the effects of anger and destruction. This leads to compassion, guiding us as to how to act in a world that is so beset with natural and unnatural disharmonies and disasters.

COMPASSION, SORROW, PITY

Karuṇā bhāvanā in yoga is the compassion which arises on seeing the vulnerability of life and the pain which is part of it. The Yogasūtra says that the perception of sorrow nourishes the growth of compassion.

Adbhuta: astonishment, wonder, amazement

This sthāyi bhāva is established by being amazed at the unexpected, when wonderful things appear and break the flow of reality. Astonishment is a driving force that pushes us to look beyond the limits of our personal self and understand phenomena that our limited sensory powers cannot. It makes us raise our heads high – not to feel personally emboldened, but to look at the greatness and complexity of life and creation with awe and wonder. The emotional experience of astonishment is stimulated by courage.

ASTONISHMENT, WONDER, AMAZEMENT

In nāṭya, the wonderful world of the thousands of Indian gods is a source of inspiration and wonderment. For a person practising yoga, the reflection on the unstained, limitless and original wisdom, called īśvara helps them to rise beyond human limitations and find a strong personal faith.

Bhayānaka: fear, fright, anxiety

Encounters with the unknown may give rise to the sthāyi bhāva of fear. In day-to-day life, fear shows us our limits and keeps us aware of forces higher than us. It prevents us from overestimating our personal power or knowledge and strengthens our understanding of interdependency. Therefore, it also has a role in our spiritual growth. It creates attention and watchfulness. It makes us aware of the things which will lead us into decay, destruction or death, and is therefore linked to the emotion of disgust.

FEAR, FRIGHT, ANXIETY

The supreme female power Kālī creates fear in us when she stretches out her tongue and drinks the blood of the demons. On a spiritual path, fear helps us remain aware of the limits of human willpower and to learn to surrender.

Bhāvas and modern science

We can enhance this view with modern science, which is the system of knowledge upon which a large part of our life today is based. The philosophy of Descartes has had a profound influence on modern thinking. Its abyssal separation of body and mind deludes us into thinking that suffering coming from emotional upheavals might exist separately from the body. It entices us into thinking that we can delve into the luxury of emotions when they are pleasant and suffer them as an unholy intrusion when they are painful. But the truth is complex: We need emotions, as much as we need to retain a balance of emotions. Some emotions are so intrinsic to us, that we need to integrate, understand and work with them. Emotionality might lead us into irrational behaviour. But the problem remains that a reduction in emotion is an equally important source of irrational behaviour.

Research studies in the modern world are drawing conclusions which are stunning when we see them from the point of view of the Nāṭyaśāstra. Since the authors of these scientific studies do not refer to the Nāṭyaśāstra, we can assume that they have arrived at their conclusions via a completely separate route. One of the key figures in modern research into the emotions is the Portuguese-American neuroscientist, Professor Antonio Damasio. His statement, *"The beginning of everything was emotion. Feeling, then, isn't a passive process"* represents a remarkable departure from the conventional view of modern science that rationality is the source of our evolution. In his 1994 book, *Descartes' Error: Emotion, Reason and the Human Brain,* he draws a distinction between what he calls primary, basic or early emotions, which are innate or 'hard-wired' (and therefore universal) and secondary or adult emotions, which derive from experience and acquired knowledge (and are thus highly individualized.) Primary emotions are associated in the brain with the limbic system, which is believed to be the physiological source of our emotions. The most fundamental emotions, known as the basic emotions, are those of anger, disgust, fear, happiness, sadness and surprise. They are indispensable in running our life, motivating and inspiring us. One can easily recognize in this list the eight basic bhāvas. The so-called "adult emotions" or "secondary emotions" of Damasio are the basis for our individual experience.

Looking back again at Nāṭyaśāstra, it is only a limited number of eight emotions, which have a subtle and intrinsic role in life and can therefore be called prime emotions.

However, our emotional life is variegated and we are confronted with many more emotions than eight. Here, the Nāṭyaśāstra speaks of transitory emotions which enhance and augment the eight prime emotions.

What are transitory emotions?

Transitory emotions are like spices which heighten the 'taste' of a prime emotion. We feel proud, when we are moved by courage, a prime emotion. We feel jealous, when we are deeply in love. Here pride and jealousy are transitory emotions, because they would vanish, if the state of courage or love was not moving us deeply. Nāṭyaśāstra mentions thirty-three transitory emotions which play a role in us:

> *Despondency, weakness, suspicion, jealousy, intoxication, weariness, indolence, depression, distraction, delusion, recollection, contentment, bashfulness, inconsistency, joy, excitement, stupefaction, arrogance, despair, impatience, sleep, loss of memory, dreaming, wakening, indigestion, pretension, fierceness, understanding, sickness, insanity, death, fright and deliberation are the 33 transitory emotions.* – *Nāṭyaśāstra VI 18-2)*

It is very helpful to learn to differentiate between the transitory and the prime emotions. The transitory emotions are not merely transitory, they are also not strongly rooted in our psyche. However, in spite of lacking deep roots, they can influence us immensely and we may get lost in trying to deal with the transitory emotions. That is why it becomes necessary to delve into the source and meaning of the prime emotions.

Unfortunately, we often confuse a transitory emotion such as pride with a prime emotion like courage. We also confuse jealousy with love, frustration with fear, haughtiness with anger, indifference with disgust, and so on. If a strong emotion like jealousy consumes us day and night, we may even conclude that it is an essential and permanent emotional state. Such a false conclusion may lead to the misunderstanding, that by leaving love behind, we can counter the effect of jealousy. Jealousy, however, may hover in the proximity of another prime emotion like courage or fear too. If we are dominated by greed, jealousy, envy, pride or any of the other transitory emotions, we may tend to think that we can get rid of these unruly emotions by leaving behind love, fear or courage. But then, these are prime emotions with deep roots in our psyche, we cannot rid ourselves of them. It is only by dealing with and developing them based on calmness, that we will be able to handle them or any transitory emotion.

Paying too much attention to these insubstantial, fleeting emotions can obscure the substrata of the prime emotions; it will then be like looking into a broken mirror – rather than seeing ourselves, we will only be seeing the damaged glass surface.

Disharmony of mental activities
will influence all our perception and
give us a scattered image of our self.

– *Yogasūtra 1.4*

The roles of prime and transitory emotions

Deep and meaningful inner experiences correspond with prime emotions only, not with the innumerable transitory emotions. We experience no direct inner bhāva of the intense feelings of jealousy, longing or lust as such; whereas we do for love, courage or anger. It is love that brings up jealousy, longing and lust. None of these would exist without love. If we do not relate to the inner bhāva of love, jealousy will be meaningless. It might grow like a parasite, but will not only serve no purpose, it will also ruin our mental and physical wellbeing. Here, love alone has a bhāva which can lead to a distinct experience, which we call the rasa, or essence. The eight prime emotions as well as śānta can be experienced as rasa.

The transitory emotions heighten our emotional life and impress upon us the role played by prime emotions. In this sense they are important. However, giving too much importance to fleeting and transitory emotions is dangerous. They will subdue the prime emotions and prevent their unfolding. We may then never come to the taste, the underlying rasa, which alone can give us insight into the situation we are dealing with. If we put too much salt in a dish we are preparing, we will only taste the salt, not the meal. The salt is important, but its overuse destroys the taste.

> *Just as various ingredients and spices blend together*
> *to make a delicious dish, the various varieties of emotions*
> *will give rise to rasa, the emotional experience.*
> *– Nāṭyaśāstra 6.35*

To put int in other words, an excessive dose of the transitory emotions will spoil the taste. There will be no experience of Rasa when the prime emotions are dominated by the transitory ones.

> *No emotional experiences can arise*
> *without the prime emotion and*

no prime emotion will be manifested
without the emotional experiences.
– Nāṭyaśāstra 6.36

Of course, the variety of our feelings is limitless. There are feelings in us which are strongly interwoven with our egoistic tendencies, like greed or self-love. These tendencies in us are not to be confused with bhāvas and rasas. They need to be studied separately and are explained in the next chapter.

The structure of the rasas

The nine rasas have a structure that will help us understand them, and thereby all our emotions. One can summarize the structure as follows:

1. **Prime emotion**

   Eight rasas are each linked to a PRIME EMOTION, sthāyi bhava, which is its core. Śānta rasa it is not really an emotion, but the state of calmness.

2. **Basis**

   Each rasa has many supporting factors, ālambana-vibhāvas. They kindle the prime emotions and make them grow stronger, thereby building their BASIS. For example, duality is the basis which kindles love.

3. **Enhancers**

   Each rasa has also uddīpana vibhāvas or ENHANCERS. These enhance the prime emotion. For example, moonlight or walks in beautiful gardens enhance the emotion of love.

TERMINOLOGY

1 PRIME EMOTION
2 BASIS
3 DISTINCT QUALITY
4 TRANSISTORY EMOTIONS
5 VISIBLE SIGNS
6 INVOLUNTARY SIGNS
7 ENHANCERS

4. **Transitory emotions**

   Each rasa has a spectrum of TRANSITORY EMOTIONS, the sañcārī bhāvas, which hover around it and contribute to the complexity of our emotional life. For example, jealousy hovers around love.

5. **Visible signs**

   Each rasa produces VISIBLE SIGNS in us, the anubhāvas, some of which are physical and others mental. For example, dreaminess or anxiety is a visible sign of love.

6. **Involuntary signs**

   Each rasa can produce INVOLUNTARY SIGNS, the sāttvika bhāvas, like blushing or sweating, which are reactions beyond our control. An involuntary and uncontrollable sign of love for instance is goose bumps. Some of the involuntary signs encountered in the nine rasas are: stupor, perspiration, goose bumps, choking of voice, trembling, loss of pallor, tears, loss of balance and becoming unconscious.

7. **Distinct quality**

   One could further say that each of the prime emotion has a DISTINCT QUALITY or lakṣaṇa through which it acquires a purpose and larger meaning. The purpose of love, for example, is to enjoy the object of love and arrive at a union with it.

Now we shall take a detailed look at each of the eight prime emotional experiences as they are understood and portrayed in the Nāṭyaśāstra.

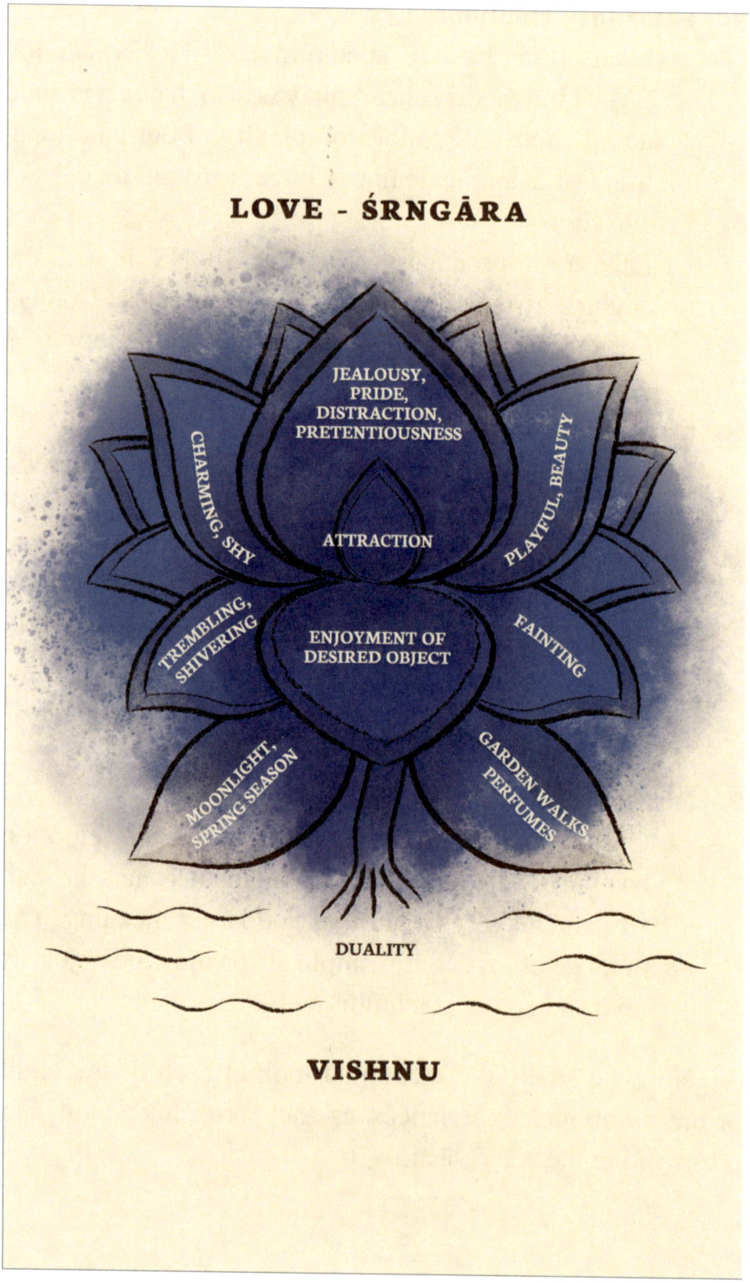
LOVE - ŚRNGĀRA
JEALOUSY, PRIDE, DISTRACTION, PRETENTIOUSNESS
CHARMING, SHY
PLAYFUL, BEAUTY
ATTRACTION
TREMBLING, SHIVERING
ENJOYMENT OF DESIRED OBJECT
FAINTING
MOONLIGHT, SPRING SEASON
GARDEN WALKS, PERFUMES
DUALITY
VISHNU

LOVE - Śṛṅgāra

Under the spell of attraction
the mood of śṛṅgāra is awakened
through the flowers of the different seasons,
the beauty of dress and ornament,
closeness to people whom we love, poetry,
and walking through parks and gardens.
– *Nāṭyaśāstra 6.47-48*

Śṛṅgāra is erotic love. The feeling for beauty develops the mood of śṛṅgāra. The senses become heightened when we are in love with another human being. His or her beauty, the way he or she is, what he or she is thinking – these become the constant subject of our thoughts. The lover acquires a glow, his or her behaviour becomes gentle and the mind gets fixed to the goal, and close to the person who is loved.

PRIME EMOTION: Ratitvam – enjoying being in love, which prevents the lover from losing sight of the object of love.

BASIS: Duality is the basis of love. The attraction of two people who fall in love with each other comes out of their oppositeness.

ENHANCERS: The enhancing factors which make love grow are the spring season, nights in moonlight, beautiful objects, walks through parks, scented things, etc.

TRANSITORY EMOTIONS: as many as 33 transitory emotions may get awakened by love, including weakness, jealousy, anger, distraction, pride, insecurity, pretentiousness, etc. Insecurity sets in, because love's aim is too far; depression arises because the separation from the lover is too long; jealousy arises because the conviction in one's own power of attraction diminishes, etc. Whenever these transitory emotions begin to dominate, we need to keep the prime emotion and the purpose behind the love constantly in mind. Neither is it appropriate to set the mind on the fleeting emotions too much, nor are they suitable themes for meditation. This does not mean that we ignore them. Rather, they make us aware that there is a prime emotion which is goading us to seek union.

VISIBLE SIGNS: Love has different visible signs. The characteristics of people in love are: being charmed, courageous, shy or excited, playful, beautiful, etc.

INVOLUNTARY SIGNS: The involuntary signs that the emotion of love produces in us are: blushing, sweating, getting goose bumps, change of voice, etc. We try to hide them because they reveal too clearly our emotional state to others, but we cannot. Giving in to the involuntary signs of a rasa is important for this can intensify the bhāva in us and bring us towards our inner goals. One whose voice trembles, who cries, shivers or faints might be close to the state of ecstasy and come to the ultimate form of love, which is the loving surrender of the individual soul to its divine cosmic source.

DISTINCT QUALITY: The central quality of love is, enjoying the object of love by achieving union with it. Love is therefore regarded as the emotion that brings human beings close to their spiritual aspirations. That is, love can lead us to devotion. It is ultimately this love in the form of devotion that can help us overcome the limitations of the 'I' and be in a love that is not dependent on a human being, but is set free to reach out to all beings. Through such deep-seated devotional love, one can see the entire world in one object. The personal love which one felt for another individual human being can become the basis for seeing the eternal Self in the other person. Then the ultimate purpose of love is fulfilled, duality overcome and union attained.

Love, śṛṅgāra-rasa, is represented by Vishnu and has the colour light green.

> *If we focus our attention on a theme and remain at it, we slowly see beyond the outer layers of the theme, come to its subtle aspects and ultimately to its core, thereby developing ānanda, deep fulfilment and letting go of the 'I'.* – *Yogasūtra 1.17*

Reflection

Love was there before us and will be there after we are gone. It is an emotion that does not belong to anyone. It is a universal force that brings opposites together. It is futile to fight against the many-faceted fleeting movements around love and try to reduce it to a uniform and simplified state which we visualize as the true state of love. Love is complex: it will always carry a personal note to it.

However, devotion to an ideal is an inherent feeling in every human being. It can dissolve the feeling of 'I' and make love all-pervasive. This transforms the way we perceive the object of love. Love is linked to bhakti – total devotion helps us respect love's divine nature. It helps realize that the beloved is a part of the divine itself and that when we surrender to the one, we surrender to all.

> *Devotion leads us to the highest state of yoga.*
> – *Yogasūtra 2.45*

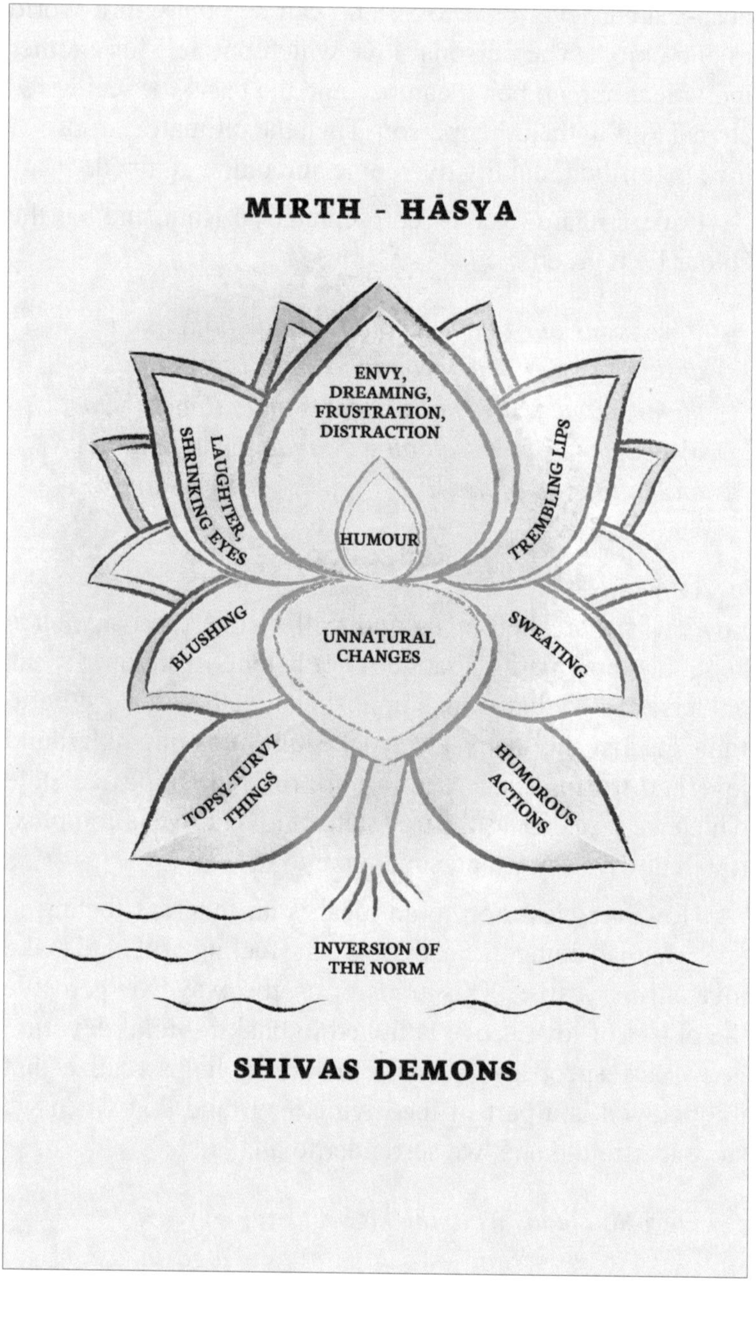
MIRTH - HĀSYA
ENVY,
DREAMING,
FRUSTRATION,
DISTRACTION
LAUGHTER,
SHRINKING EYES
TREMBLING LIPS
HUMOUR
BLUSHING
UNNATURAL
CHANGES
SWEATING
TOPSY-TURVY
THINGS
HUMOROUS
ACTIONS
INVERSION OF
THE NORM
SHIVAS DEMONS

AMUSEMENT - Hāsya

Through unsuited clothing, strange hair-style,
strange behaviour or gestures and
words without sense
which make others laugh
the mood of hāsya is produced. – *Nāṭyaśāstra 6.50*

Hāsya or amusement brings us into the emotion of lightness and mirth. It leads us to the question: "Is what we are seeing really the truth?" Turning things upside down or seeing them from unusual angles is the nature of a clown: it brings out truths which were hidden before.

Indian mythology abounds in instances where things are turned upside down. The world of the gods is full of improbable images: Ganesha the elephant god rides on a mouse, Vishnu sleeps on a snake, out of his navel appears a lotus in which the creator sits and smiles. The arts constantly provoke these gods with jokes and ridicule. A dancer will speak to her or his god asking him with gestures: "O, you must have become tired or ashamed of all your amorous games and therefore hidden yourself within a stone statue in this temple!", says the Kannada poet Kanakadasa in one of his evocative songs in praise of Krishna, "Jagado dharaka…"

Humour, according to the Nāṭyaśāstra, grows out of love and the erotic sentiment.

When we let go of the norms that we cling to, we help hāsya develop. Our perception of reality is mostly filled with our illusions and expectations. To look at life as a play in which the joker can replace all the existing figures will help us develop a distance from the way things appear to us.

On the contrary, finding fault with others comes out of a feeling that we are in the right. It ensues out of frustration. Frustration is a sañcāri bhāva (transitory emotion) of both love and amusement.

Nothing is superfluous.
Certain things may be evident to us
and therefore closed matters,
but not necessarily for others too.

– *Yogasūtra 2.22*

PRIME EMOTION: Being humorous and mirthful is the prime emotion of amusement.

BASIS: Happenings which do not conform to the norm make amusement grow.

ENHANCERS: The enhancing factors are topsy-turvy and humorous actions.

TRANSITORY EMOTIONS: The transitory emotions are weakness, envy, dreaming, frustration, indolence, distraction etc.

VISIBLE SIGNS: Laughter, shrinking eyes or trembling lips are some of the signs which become visible when we get into a state of amusement.

INVOLUNTARY SIGNS: Blushing and sweating.

DISTINCT QUALITY: Enjoying the state of amusement is important, because it helps us to learn to perceive reality differently.

The colour of hāsya is white and its godly representatives are the Pramathas, the grotesque-looking watchmen of Shiva.

Reflection

Humour has a significant role in our emotional life, it frees us from our preconceptions and helps us to adjust to the unexpected in everyday life. Humour takes away our obsession with what we *think* is truth, and helps us look at our own imperfections.

If we recognize an object,
it does not mean necessarily
that what we see is the truth.
It merely indicates that we
wish to deal with this object
and that it has moved close enough
for us to be able to deal with it.

– *Yogasūtra 4.17*

Disgust - Bībhatsa

By seeing disgusting things,
disturbing taste, terrible smells,
dreadful touches or awful noises
which prevent the mind from being calm,
the emotion of disgust develops.

– *Nāṭyaśāstra 6.73*

When we witness disgusting things, we do not remain quiet. We speak passionately about how awful this or that is, and thereby move mentally away from it. In this way we take a standpoint about things we do not like and things we wish to distance ourselves from.

We feel ashamed about the horrible deeds of crime, dishonesty and other violent perversions of mankind. Such a sense of shame and disgust helps us to not identify ourselves

DISGUST - BĪBHATSA
REVOLT, DISTRACTION, APPREHENSION,- DESPAIR
CONTRACTING BODY, EYES AND MOUTH
VOMITING
DISGUST
STUPOR
REALIZING THE BLEMISHES
SHIVERING, CRAMPS
HEARING, SEEING OR SMELLING BAD THINGS
COMING INTO CONTACT WITH SLIMY THINGS
UNDESIRABLE THINGS
MAHĀKĀLA

with these things, keep a distance and not get too involved with them. Such an emotion does not mean that we look down on something, hold hatred or pass judgements. We merely do not want to have a part in things for which we feel disgust. The spiritual meaning behind feeling ashamed or disgusted is to clearly spot the inconsistency in life and consequently develop a dispassionate and non-avaricious attitude towards it. This has the power to dissolve illusions about the perfection or permanence of things and life.

If we practice purity deeply,
we will develop disgust towards the physical,
which is impermanent and
remain untouched by the illusions,
with which people around us influence us.
– Yogasūtra 2.40

We practice such a dispassion not by covering up or ignoring the unpleasant things but identifying them as they are. Only then can we prevent ourselves from falling into a negative outlook or becoming judgemental and merely staying mentally detached. We can then concentrate on matters we like to be part of. In this way the mind purifies itself for the experience of love. According to the Nāṭyaśāstra disgust is the polar opposite of love.

PRIME EMOTION: to feel disgusted about undesirable things.

BASIS: is the undesirable, which forces itself into our perception.

ENHANCING FACTORS: Hearing, seeing or smelling bad things, coming into contact with slimy things.

TRANSITORY EMOTIONS: Revolt, distraction, apprehension, disease, despair and feeling intoxicated are some of the transitory emotions around disgust.

VISIBLE SIGNS are the contracting of the body, the eyes and the mouth, vomiting, etc.

INVOLUNTARY SIGNS: shivering, cramps, stupor and getting goose bumps.

DISTINCT QUALITY: The central quality or laksaṇa here is that disgust helps us to realize the imperfection or blemishes in the things around us and thereby develop a non-avaricious and detached attitude towards them.

In distancing ourselves from unwanted factors, we might be overcome by a transitory emotion like feeling paralysed or being depressed. Here we have to divert our attention to the prime emotion to understand what it is really that we need to distance ourselves from.

Mahākāla, the Lord of the eternal Time symbolises this emotion and its colour is blue.

By cleansing ourselves and
thereby distancing ourselves from disgusting things,
the mind will become pure, positive attitudes will develop,
the senses will become sharpened
and the capacity to see the inner Self will grow.

– *Yogasūtra 2.41*

Reflection

Decaying things evoke the feeling of disgust. Decay shows the impermanence of living objects. We become aware of the inconsistency of life and are therefore reminded to maintain a distance from it.

Disgust is an emotional force: it creates an attitude of not wanting to contribute to or enhance decay. With this attitude we will also stay away from causing destruction to living beings.

FEAR - Bhayānaka

When we hear dreadful noises,
meet frightening people, battle,
enter desolate houses or dark forests,
or when we do wrong to our elders,
the emotion of fear will arise.

– *Nāṭyaśāstra 6.69*

If we fall into the clutches of fear, we tend to become scared of objects or people, even if they are of no threat to us. We lose trust in the things we had otherwise trusted, faith in the people in whom we have otherwise had faith. Deep within us we have an inborn tendency to trust. Faith is the stuff our psyche is made of. Inasmuch, we are bound to be able to relink to that faith deep within us. The Bhagavadgītā says that the human being is imbued in faith, it is the fabric from which he or she is woven: *Sraddhā mayo'yam puruṣah* (Bhagavadgītā 17.3).

The experience of fear can then become a motivation for us to search for that lost inner faith.

According to the Nāṭyaśāstra, fear comes out of the emotion of disgust.

Faith gives us strength,
sharp memory and clarity.
Or, to put it in other words,

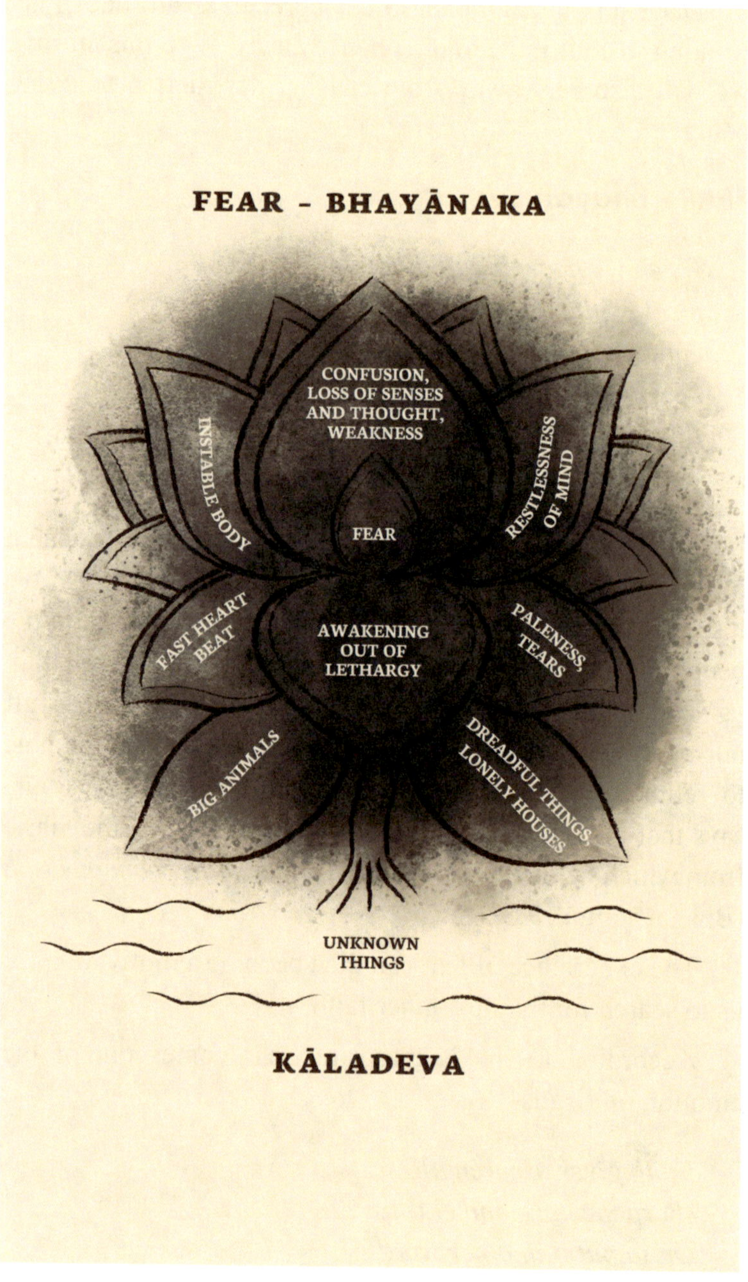
FEAR - BHAYĀNAKA
CONFUSION, LOSS OF SENSES AND THOUGHT, WEAKNESS
INSTABLE BODY
RESTLESSNESS OF MIND
FEAR
FAST HEART BEAT
AWAKENING OUT OF LETHARGY
PALENESS, TEARS
BIG ANIMALS
DREADFUL THINGS, LONELY HOUSES
UNKNOWN THINGS
KĀLADEVA

faith will nourish us with energy
to remember our past experiences
and move away from ignorance.

– *Yogasūtra 1.20*

PRIME EMOTION: fear

BASIS: The basis for fear is the anticipation of undesirable, unknown occurrences.

TRANSITORY EMOTIONS: the transitory emotions are trembling, confusion, loss of senses and thought, weakness etc.

ENHANCING FACTORS: the enhancing factors are terrible deeds, big animals and dreadful things that happen around us.

VISIBLE SIGNS: unstable movements of the body and restlessness of thought.

INVOLUNTARY SIGNS: dryness of mouth, stiffness of joints, rapid heartbeat, tears, fainting, and paleness of face.

DISTINCT QUALITY: to awaken us out of a lethargic and indifferent attitude, so that we start moving out towards greater acceptance of life.

Fear is associated with/represented by the God of Time, Kāladeva and the colour black.

Reflection

If we step on a thorn and have no fear of an infection, we might not remove the thorn, develop an indifferent attitude towards dangers and get into trouble. If we make a mistake because we did not have proper knowledge of a situation and hurt others, we regret it and become sad. Fear has an important role to play, promoting caution in our actions and

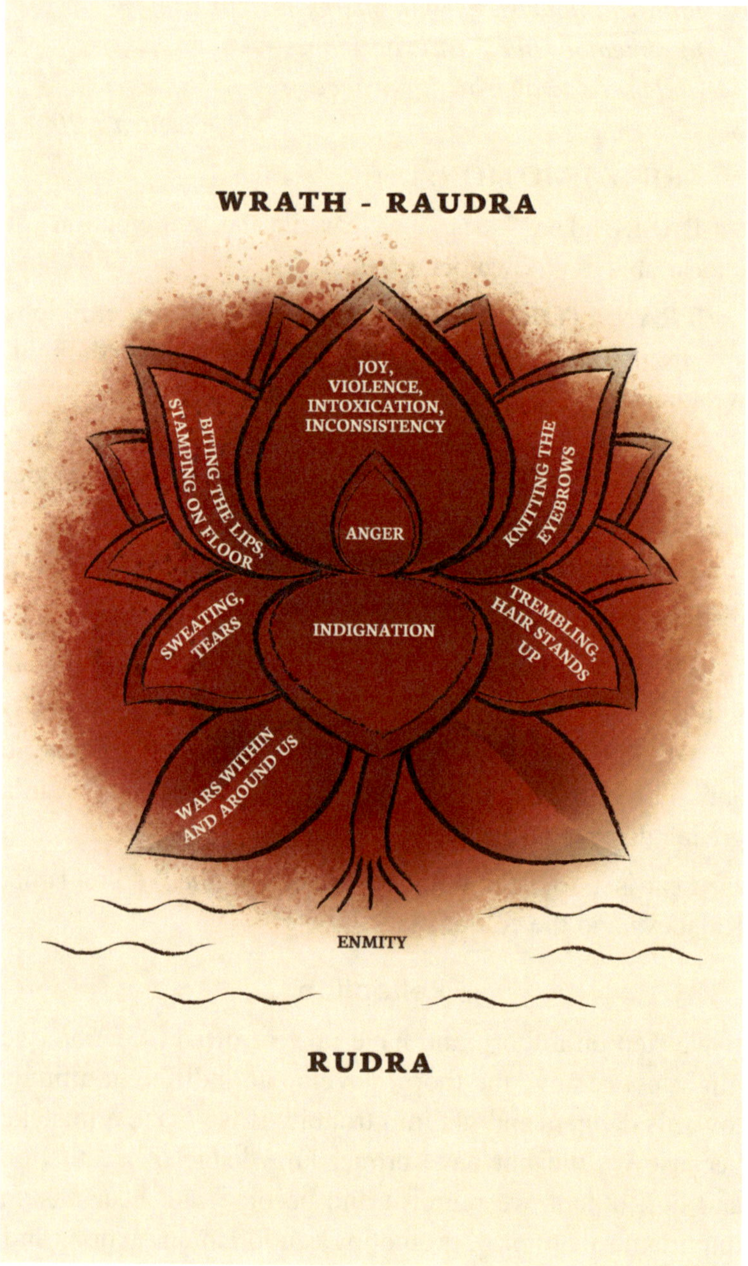
WRATH - RAUDRA
JOY, VIOLENCE, INTOXICATION, INCONSISTENCY
BITING THE LIPS, STAMPING ON FLOOR
KNITTING THE EYEBROWS
ANGER
SWEATING, TEARS
INDIGNATION
TREMBLING, HAIR STANDS UP
WARS WITHIN AND AROUND US
ENMITY
RUDRA

therefore respect for life. Fear will prompt us to not repeat our mistakes.

If, however, fear weakens our faith, we have to be watchful. This will not happen if we have experienced the rasa of love, for faith and love are linked to each other like mother and child.

> The *Sraddha Suktam,* of the *Taittirīya Brāhmaṇa* declares, *"Śraddhā kāmasya mātaram"* (Faith is the mother of love).

ANGER - Krodha

> *A mighty energy that can establish justice*
> *Through violent actions,*
> *tumult of battles and the like,*
> *the emotion of anger will be born.*
>
> – *Nāṭyaśāstra. 6. 46 -76*

We often associate anger with uncontrollable passion because of the energy it brings into our veins. When we are angry, our blood circulation seems to be agitated and a strong impetus for action arises. Anger seems to spur us to gain the space which we have lost. Anger can help overcome hindrances and create space for a new beginning.

Anger is present in everybody's life. It reveals that there is injustice and that an imbalance is disturbing our environment. It is, at its core, more than just a personal fury. Many philosophical and religious schools of thought speak of not getting angry at all. But anger is a valid human sentiment. Also, it is only by channelling anger that compassion can develop.

Anger is a divine force like all the other eight prime emotions. We cannot decide to have or not have it. Of course, it is not good to hurt other beings on the basis of anger. Inflicting damage on others is not the goal of anger at all.

Involvement with the worldly life is important,
for it gives us the impetus to
differentiate between reality and illusion.
– Yogasūtra 2.23

PRIME EMOTION: The prime emotion is anger or wrathfulness.

BASIS: It is provoked by the indignation we feel towards an offence committed by another person.

ENHANCERS: The enhancing factors are the wars around and within us.

TRANSITORY EMOTIONS: Various emotions begin to show up when there is anger, such as pride, joy, violence, intoxication, fierceness, jealousy, inconsistency etc.

VISIBLE SIGNS: biting the lips, knitting the eyebrows, flourishing weapons, stamping on the floor, etc.

INVOLUNTARY SIGNS: the hair stands up, sweat and tears flow, change of voice, trembling and change of colour.

DISTINCT QUALITY: We get activated by the sight of injustice and draw energy to remove it. That is the distinct effect that anger carries with it.

In life there is anger that is directed towards parents, to develop our own views. There is anger towards one's own children, to help them learn their limits. There is anger towards companions, and this concerns discovering truth. And there is anger against enemies to protect oneself.

Rudra represents anger, and it is symbolized by the colour red.

Reflection

We have to accept that there are opponents in life. Sometimes it is an individual being, sometimes certain people who oppose us or situations which hinder our lives. When we become aware of them, anger can arise. Grumpiness, displeasure, frustration over personal matters or the rise of violent urges is not anger. Anger is a force which demands our respect as it belongs to the gods.

Though many religious scriptures teach us to avoid anger, they also speak of the anger of gods and great kings. Anger can establish fairness. It will not go out of bounds, if we remind ourselves that its goal ultimately is to establish justice. At its root, anger is there to instigate action, never to provoke us into aggression. If our personal goal is strong, it will deflect us from bringing out our energy aggressively towards the person before us, and help focus it towards this personal goal.

The disturbances of the mind can be resolved by
singular devotion to a subject of our choice.
– Yogasūtra 1.32

COMPASSION - Kāruṇya

The emotion of compassion
comes into existence through
the loss of beloved ones,
on hearing of cruel actions,
due to sadness over the death
of people we know, etc. *– Nāṭyaśāstra 6.62*

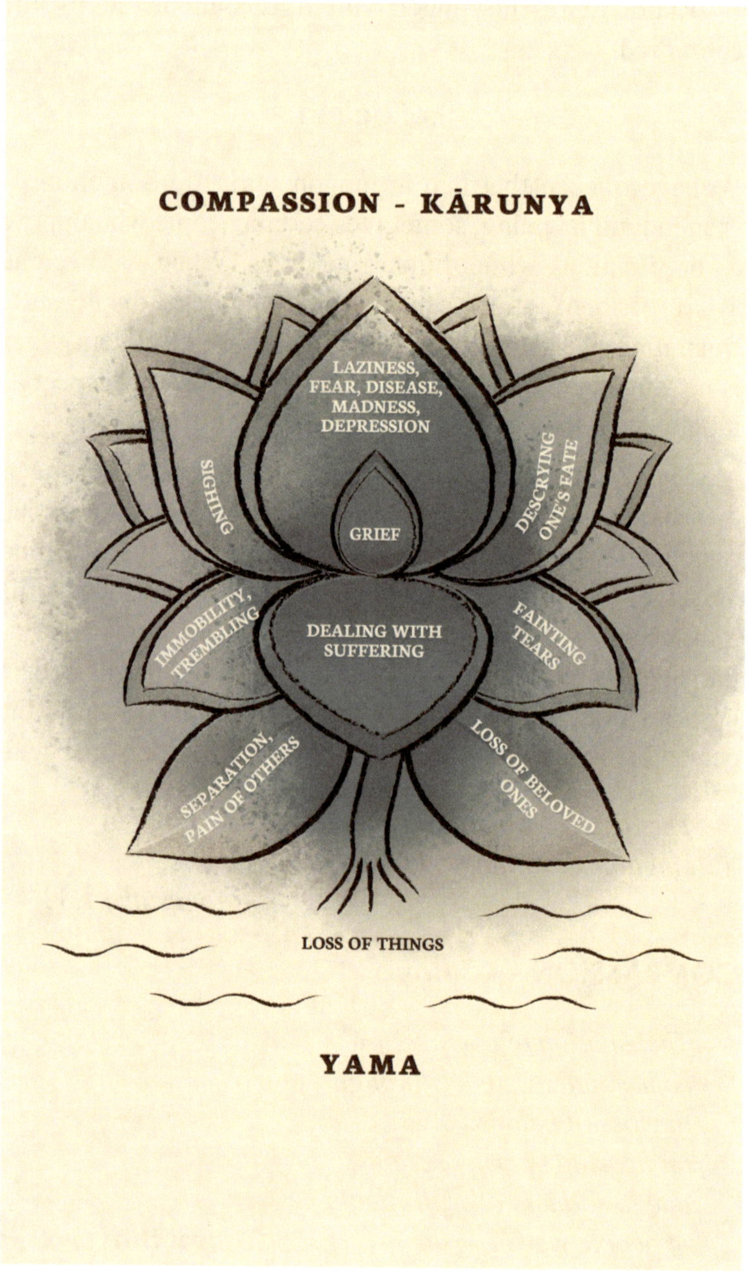
COMPASSION - KĀRUNYA
LAZINESS, FEAR, DISEASE, MADNESS, DEPRESSION
SIGHING
DESCRYING ONE'S FATE
GRIEF
IMMOBILITY, TREMBLING
DEALING WITH SUFFERING
FAINTING TEARS
SEPARATION, PAIN OF OTHERS
LOSS OF BELOVED ONES
LOSS OF THINGS
YAMA

Compassion is a poignant emotion which develops on the basis of sorrow. It fills us with empathy for the suffering in the world and helps us to understand suffering.

It is a love where the self finds fulfilment in feeding and attending to the suffering person without expecting any reward in return. Compassion which is not linked to sorrow arises from a condescending sense of pity or self-pity. The compassionate person, by contrast, consoles and gives comfort. It is identical with the karuṇā bhāvanā in yoga.

The attack of an enemy brings about sorrow. Compassion is that reaction to sorrow where we do not become alarmed, or fall into despair, but help. It is an emotion that makes us act to prevent harm. It is the emotion of wise and saintly people. Moreover, it is the power of karuṇā, which reduces the suffering in the other person.

According to the Nāṭyaśāstra, compassion arises out of anger:

The passage of time,
habits, memories, inner conflicts
all these provoke suffering to arise.
Suffering is everywhere. The wise know it.

But one can take steps today,
to lessen the suffering of tomorrow.

– *Yogasūtra 2.15 & 2.16*

PRIME EMOTION: The prime emotion is sorrow, which feeds compassion.

BASIS: It grows when we recognize the suffering in the world.

ENHANCING FACTORS: Seeing the pain of others, separation and loss of beloved ones and things.

TRANSITORY EMOTIONS: Sleeplessness, laziness, fear, weakness, despair, disease, madness, thoughtfulness, depression, anxiety, etc.

VISIBLE SIGNS: Sighing, falling on the ground, descrying one's fate etc.

INVOLUNTARY SIGNS: Tears, change of voice, trembling, fainting and immobility.

DISTINCT QUALITY: This emotion ultimately enables us to become capable of dealing with suffering.

Compassion is represented by the God of Death, Yama, and the colour grey.

Reflection

Loss is a constant feature of everybody's life, as nothing is permanent in this world. Therefore, the wise man is full of compassion for all living beings, before and after they experience the loss.

We often become helpless when problems arise and people around us suffer. By developing compassion, we find the strength to handle suffering and act towards reducing it. To develop compassion is the surest way of dealing with anger and giving rein to the energy it draws out of us. This attitude can help us mitigate the aggressiveness within us and benefit our surroundings.

A person rooted in non-violence quells the aggression in his surroundings.

– Yogasūtra 2.35

COURAGE - Vīra

By looking at an enthusiastic,
motivated and optimistic person,
who has presence of mind
and will not get deluded,
the emotion of valour is born.

– *Nāṭyaśāstra 6.67*

Valour or courage is not an emotion belonging to warriors or fighters alone. It is also the emotional state of artists, saints, seers, doctors, explorers and all those who identify themselves strongly with the role they have committed to in their lives. Valour or courage is a precondition to becoming a protective mother or a responsible father, or a human being with a positive outlook on life. It helps us to forge ahead to the limits of our capacities, to have the nerve to probe beyond the limit which timidity might set. It is a basis for all the development we strive for, whether in the outer or inner world. Since courage links us strongly with our aim and helps us stay committed to our path, focusing on our goals with determination, it is an emotion which is suited for meditation.

To be determined means,
to be constantly focussed
towards one goal for a long time,
with a positive outlook of mind and
without causing harm to others.

– *Yogasūtra 1.13 & 1.14*

PRIME EMOTION: Feeling energized and valorous is the prime emotion.

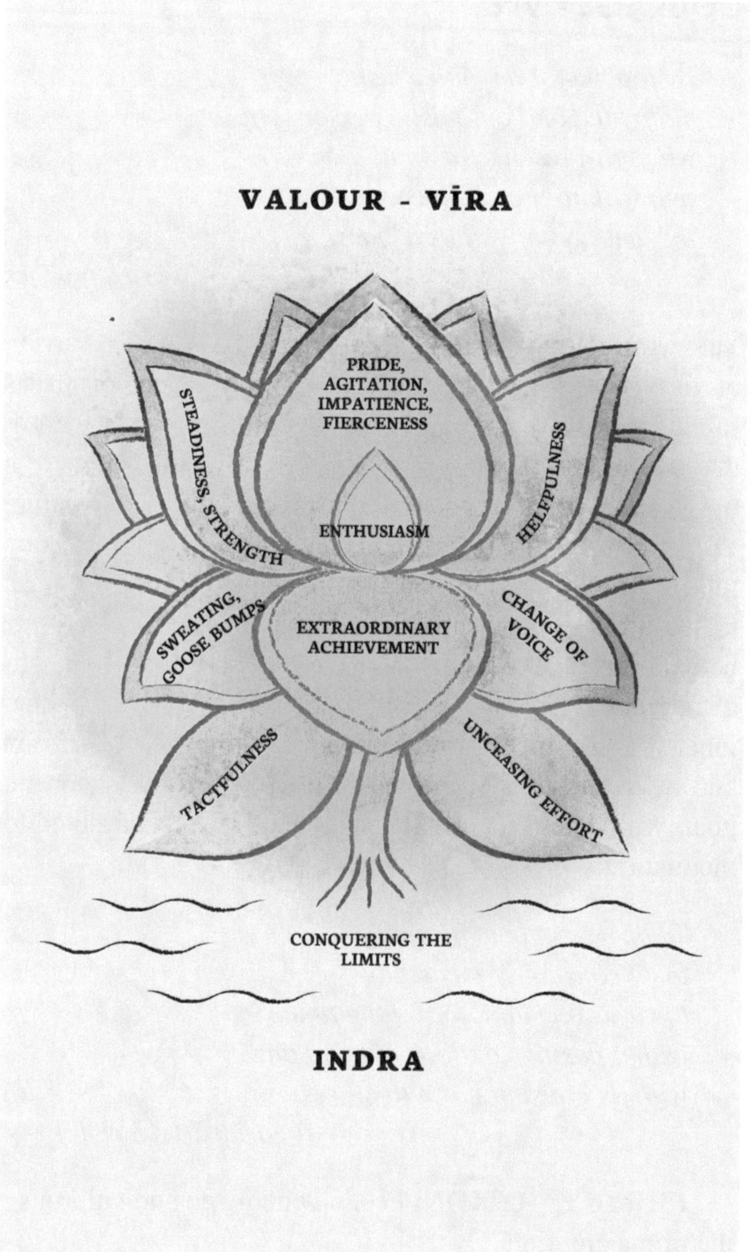
VALOUR - VĪRA
PRIDE,
AGITATION,
IMPATIENCE,
FIERCENESS
STEADINESS, STRENGTH
HELPFULNESS
ENTHUSIASM
SWEATING,
GOOSE BUMPS
EXTRAORDINARY
ACHIEVEMENT
CHANGE OF
VOICE
TACTFULNESS
UNCEASING EFFORT
CONQUERING THE
LIMITS
INDRA

BASIS: Knowledge of our limits, that which lies unconquered beyond these limits, and the desire to conquer them.

ENHANCING FACTORS: Tactfulness, actions pertaining to conquering and unceasing efforts.

TRANSITORY EMOTIONS: Envy, pride, contentment, agitation, impatience, fierceness, confidence.

VISIBLE SIGNS: Steadiness, boldness of mind, absence of the fear of losing something, strength, readiness to help others.

INVOLUNTARY SIGNS: Goose bumps, sweating, change of colour in the face and change of voice.

DISTINCT QUALITY: Courage helps us achieve that which is above the ordinary.

The god representing this emotion is Indra and the colour is bright yellow.

Reflection

Some human beings exude authority due to their inner graciousness, which gives them greatness. There are other people who are born into families of leaders. But there are some who acquire leadership characteristics by developing this emotional state.

To develop visions and reach goals, we need courage. Courage helps people teach and guide others. The message indicated by the above is clear: do not strive for power or powerful positions without being able to experience the bhāva of courage, and being backed by it.

WONDERSTRUCK - ADBHUTA
DELUSION, EXCITEMENT, ANXIETY
WAVING ARMS, OPENING THE EYES WIDE
DANCING, DROPPING INHIBITIONS
AMAZEMENT
TRANCE, AGITATION
TRANSCENDENCE
CHOKING OF VOICE
IMPRESSIVE ARCHITECTURE, MAGICAL THINGS
HUMANS WITH EXTRAORDINARY SKILLS
THE DIVINE
BRAHMA

ASTONISHMENT - Adbhuta

All words we hear and actions we perceive,
which go beyond the limits of the normal experience,
result in the emotion of amazement.

– Nāṭyaśāstra 4.75

At times we wish to rise beyond the world of reasoning and leave the intellect behind. We have a longing to see and connect with a force that is not of this world. The desire to experience wonder in one's lifetime is there in many people. This desire is the hope that one can be liberated from the material world. Being open to wonder and astonishment results in a strong pull towards meditation. It means we are prepared to let the unexpected take over our over-expectant mind.

According to the Nāṭyaśāstra astonishment arises out of courage.

PRIME EMOTION: The feeling of astonishment is the prime emotion.

BASIS: It is our innate longing to experience the divine or the transcendence.

ENHANCING FACTORS: Astonishment grows at the sight of beautiful gardens, impressive architecture, seeing and experiencing magical things or meeting human beings with extraordinary skills and powers.

TRANSITORY EMOTIONS: Some of the transitory feelings which accompany it are delusion, anxiety, excitement.

VISIBLE SIGNS: Reactions such as dropping of inhibitions, waving the arms, opening the eyes wide, clapping the hands, and dancing with the arms stretched out.

INVOLUNTARY SIGNS: Being agitated, getting into a trance or the choking of the voice can happen when we enter into this emotion.

DISTINCT QUALITY: Astonishment drives us to reach a higher state of consciousness.

The god representing this emotion is Brahma, the creator, and its colour is yellow.

Continuous practice of meditation
can lead to extraordinary results.
But these results can themselves
become hindrances, if they distract us
from the goal of transforming our consciousness.
(Yogasūtra 3.37)

Reflection

There is much more to life than meets the eye, much more to be seen than the 'I' can see. Keep your eyes wide open and take note of the wonderful things happening around you. Learn to look up and see things which are much bigger than you, much subtler and more powerful than you. This can sharpen your vision and widen your perception.

Awareness of the deep self within us leads to extraordinarily illuminated perception of the five senses. – Yogasūtra 3.36

If you get into a deep process which is mysterious and wonderful, do not get carried away by the joy and become distracted. You then lose the alertness to be open to further wonders.

CONCLUDING THOUGHTS ON BHĀVA/RASA

The eight prime emotions can be observed, understood and experienced. They are intrinsic to our nature and do not pose a threat to us. It is our task to extricate them from the horde of transitory emotions which tend to shroud them. To be able to do that, we must keep in mind that calmness, the substratum of all emotions, alone can help us experience an emotion stably. This will help us gain the experience, the taste of the emotion, the rasa. We are then capable of enjoying the emotion without being trapped in it. We can experience and profit from the strength it gives us without becoming attached to it.

But the mind is often inert or lazy, clouded or distracted. We cannot easily establish a bit of calmness in ourselves to be able to experience the emotions this way. What do we do?

In the next chapter we describe the nine hindrances in our mind, or antarāyas as Yogasūtra calls them. These hindrances are movable, if not removable. It requires some effort, but Yogasūtra also gives us ideas to deal with them.

5

ANTARĀYA

The Nine Hindrances

Antarāyas are hindrances that *appear to be* emotions. How do we differentiate between subconscious emotions which we feel and disturbing feelings which appear like emotions?

There is a confusion about the word 'feeling'. This has a lot to do with the way we use – and misuse – it. We talk of 'feeling sick', forgetting that sickness is actually an imbalance in our state of health. We 'feel' dull: dullness is a disturbance in our energy levels. We talk of feeling diffident, unaware that diffidence results from a disturbed picture of our selves. We deal with disturbances in our personality as though they were troublesome feelings. As much as there are nine emotional states, there are nine qualities in us hindering deep emotional experiences. We have to reflect upon these nine hindrances, or antarāyas, to see how they affect our nine prime emotions. Patanjali lists the antarāyas as follows:

Being unwell, unmotivated,
indecisive, impatient, idle,
distracted, confused, diffident

and unsteady are hindrances
which bring disharmony to
our mental activities.

– Yogasūtra 1.30

Antarāyas are obstacles between us and what we seek. They are there in everybody's life. Sometimes perhaps only one is present, but at other times many are. They cloud our mental activities and influence our feelings and thoughts, making it impossible for us to shed prejudices or judgements. If we remain passive, they slowly lead us into grief. If we do not tackle these hindrances, we will not come out of this grief. We instead develop a pessimistic and sarcastic outlook on life. If the situation worsens, they can influence our physical wellbeing and ultimately lead to breathlessness. Over time this tends towards suffocation and loss of control over physiological functions, and ruins our peace of mind.

If the antarāyas are active in us,
we are overpowered by suffering
and become mentally gloomy,
physically unsteady and
totally lose control of our breath.

– Yogasūtra 1.31

Vyādhi (dis-ease, being unwell): A person who is constantly occupied with his being **unwell** will not be attracted by the sight of beautiful things and therefore not experience the emotion of love.

Styāna (heaviness, being unmotivated): An **unmotivated** person will not be drawn into the emotional state of anger.

Samśaya (indecisiveness): Whoever is **indecisive** will not have the courage to go ahead with the tasks at hand.

Pramāda (impatience): An **impatient** person will not pay attention to things around them, develop a negligent attitude and close themselves off to the sorrow around them and therefore fail to develop compassion.

Ālasya (idleness): The **idle** person will become indifferent, gradually lose all resistance against influences around him and fail to feel distaste for things which are disgusting.

Avirati (distractedness): Distraction is a huge obstacle to overcome in order to reach a state of calmness.

Bhrāntidarśana (confusion): A person who is **confused** will deceive himself perpetually, fail to see the extraordinary and not know the wonderful sentiment of being astonished.

Alabdhabhūmikatva (diffidence): Someone who is **diffident** lacks self-confidence and will not be able to tackle things with lightness and therefore not appreciate humour and light-heartedness.

Anavasthitatva (unsteadiness): An **unsteady** person, not being motivated enough to overcome hurdles, will jump from task to task and avoid all confrontation with fearful events.

In these ways and more, the nine hindrances can block the emotions. However, it is the emotions themselves which can help us resolve these hindrances. In the following section we describe each hindrance and explain, through examples, the role played by emotions in tackling each one of them.

Being Unwell (Vyādhi)

Illness originates in three different ways:

- Through external influences, like bacteria or injuries which weaken us
- Through unforeseen sources such as floods and other natural calamities
- Through our own unsuitable behaviour patterns. This type of disease, based on deep-seated inclinations and disinclinations, develops slowly and surreptitiously due to mistakes we make.

Today, most of us humans are far removed from a natural way of living with a harmonious link to instincts. We may miss such harmony, but do not know what could help us re-establish it. In the absence of such a harmony, small and even insignificant discomforts start to dominate our minds and our daily life: a headache, a stomach upset and so on. It is the same way in which the transitory emotions dominate a prime one! We forget that we are connected to and are part of nature, which is always tuned to healing itself.

The loss of this connection to nature's holistic ways leads to destructive thoughts in us. It takes us to a point where we feel life imposes suffering on us and deprives us of many things. These destructive thoughts influence our natural behaviour patterns and the results are: bad food habits, lack of physical exercise and not enough rest for body and mind. This sets a vicious cycle in motion, resulting in a general lack of wellbeing. We get gradually drawn into a spiral far removed from the harmonious wheel of life.

Whatever our ailment may be, eventually what we will need to recover is faith in nature and its self-healing power. That alone can show us the path to come out of serious problems related to our wellbeing. That alone can help us understand the way in which our sickness rules over us and to activate the skills and instincts we have in order to fight our way out of sickness. Becoming aware of the harmony in nature, loving and appreciating it is a big first step.

Here the emotion of love will help. For it can evoke attraction in us, whether it is the love of nature or a similar form of love. Love can give us back our faith and resurrect our healing strength. It focuses our mind on the object of love, nourishes our faith and draws us towards the experience of oneness. Health is an integral part of this experience of oneness.

The hindrances of our mind can be overcome
by developing closeness to a human being
who has overcome difficulties in life.

– *Yogasūtra 1.37*

Being unwell weakens the feeling of attraction in us and hinders love. If we focus our mind on things which are lovable to us, we can mobilize our healing power. Whether we see beauty in nature, in a god or human being, it does not matter. The rasa of love is a healing medicine, because love enhances faith and activates our healing capacity. To have faith in our self is to have faith in nature's healing power for we are part of nature.

The thinking mind plays an important role in healing too. We have to sharpen our judgement and become aware of the things which will support our wellbeing and those that will harm it.

Faith can be blind if it shuts out judgement and makes us overestimate our own healing power. However, if judgement overpowers love, our faith can collapse. If we keep our judgement and faith in balance, we can overcome the sense of loss and being unwell.

Illustration: An excellent pair

A little boy wanted to set out to explore the wide world. His anxious grandmother sent him off with the following advice: "Sleep at night only under a tamarind tree. If you want to return home, sleep every night under a neem tree." The boy set off, keeping this in mind. Each night he slept under a tamarind tree. As the days went by, he gradually grew ill. When he became very weak, he decided to go back to his grandmother. Every night he slept under a neem tree. By and by, the boy started to feel better and was back to normal health by the time he reached his grandmother's house again. The wise old lady smiled: now he has learnt that there are things in the world which heal, and things which make us unwell (the neem is a healing tree and the air under a tamarind tree is supposed to have toxic energies.) The wise judgement of the grandmother and the innocent faith of the boy in the grandmother's advice show how emotion and thought work together in the healing process. The grandmother's concern about the wellbeing of her grandson setting out all alone too early in life, and the love and faith of the little boy for his grandmother – how beautifully these two aspects of the mind come together!

Lacking Motivation (Styāna)

Everything in the world is constantly changing: there is nothing we can permanently hold on to. However, there is a side to us which wants to have it easy. It wants us to remain where we are, does not accept change, and does not want to be part of this constant movement. It avoids challenge and effort, and clings on to things or happenings of the past. Instead of responding to what's happening around us, we become dull and indifferent. We even confuse such lethargy with equanimity or a dispassionate attitude.

If we habitually adopt such an attitude, we slowly lose our motivation. We then refuse to act unless we are assured of pleasant results. And since we have not really overcome the desire for good things, we easily become disappointed, disinterested, and sink into lethargy, endlessly preoccupied with the question: "What does all this bring me?" We are thus caught in the wheel of expectation, disappointment and disinterest, which further weakens our motivation. We then become dependent on external factors to get us back on the move or give us a reason for coming out of lethargy. This not only robs us of all motivation, but also kills our spontaneity.

Idleness is often clothed in the guise of a dispassionate attitude. It is passion alone that can move us out of an idle, indifferent or lethargic state of mind. If passion in us dissipates, the motivation to act will also weaken. It is again the emotions that can set our minds and therefore the limbs, too, in motion. The injustice around us can ignite this passion and spur us into action. Anger in its essence helps us stay alert and react to the presence of something we regard as unjust or improper. Anger can move us out of lethargy and provide us the mental agility we need to keep in step with change. Obviously, this anger will have served its purpose the moment we leave the lethargy behind. To give vent to this anger by resorting to violence would be an abuse of the emotion.

When the mind gets deeply linked
to the energy in us,
which counteracts lethargy,
we will be able to resist
every challenge that pulls us down
and even move without difficulty
over thorns, swamps or water.

– *Yogasūtra 3.39*

If we try to ignore the force which anger provides us, we may lose our energy. Anger is an emotion whose actual goal is to provide us energy, not for harming others but for fuelling our will to act. If we fear the force of anger and avoid action, we may fool ourselves into equating lethargy with calmness of mind.

Calmness helps by moderating the pace of our actions and prevents us from inflicting harm on others. But we cannot misinterpret it and thereby destroy the essence of anger. We have to let the two emotions blend together so that we do not inflict harm, remain motivated and retain our vitality.

Illustration: Śiva as Nataraja, the cosmic dancer

Śiva as Nataraja, the cosmic dancer, is a beautiful image. His body is the universe and His dance the never-ending movement of time. We are nothing but a speck of dust in this cosmic happening, which turns the future into the present and then into the past. Every motion, be it the turn of a thought or the gush of mighty winds, is a part of the dance. The idea of a personal or independent movement outside the space and time of his dance is an illusion, represented by the helpless demon on which Śiva's dancing foot is firmly placed. We have the choice to accept being part of this cosmic happening and blend gracefully into its rhythms. We have the force within us to stay conscious of the realm and rhythm of this change and avoid being trampled by it.

Being Indecisive (Samśaya)

The classic conflict between feelings and thoughts is expressed in statements like, "my heart tells me..." or "my mind says...". Indecisiveness results whenever we separate the feeling and the thinking mind. When we become unsure about the outcome of a situation, we begin to doubt our decision or become suspicious of our perception. We begin to lose our confidence and capacity for spontaneous decision and action.

We can neither bring an unclear situation entirely under control, nor can we be sure of acting without making a mistake or hurting someone, in a complex situation. The pleasant and unpleasant are both part of life. A world free of risks and a life free from mistakes could be ideal, but in the reality of our day-to-day life, this is an illusion. If we fool ourselves into believing that making a mistake and consequently hurting someone is dreadful, even if it is not intended at all, we might be conveniently excusing our indecisiveness and inaction with a seeming compassion for others. Here, we have to remind ourselves that a wrong action done with a clear intention is always better than resisting action. Is it not the order of the universe that it acts all the time? By being part of the universe, we are already in the wheel of action which supports and sustains the universe. By refraining from conscious action, we do not really stop acting. We may in fact be acting without bringing our emotions and awareness into the action.

Only when we begin to shed our fear of what we call a wrong action and realize the danger of a false concern, will we have the courage to rise above our limitations and take a decision. Only then will we find the strength to protect those for whose welfare we had concern, before we decided to act. The decisiveness will eventually help us develop the instinctive feeling for right action.

The role of courage in countering indecisiveness

The joy in taking up a task and seeing it through to the end is a strong emotional experience. This indicates and manifests as valour or courage and drives us into action. In a balanced state of mind, we would be valiant and motivate ourselves into taking decisions courageously.

> *If we reflect deeply,*
> *why certain things we do*
> *are successful and certain*
> *other things take their own time,*
> *we will understand what the*
> *outcome of our life could be.*
>
> – *Yogasūtra 3.22*

Often in life it is either others that dictate our decisions or circumstances do. For instance, we are forced to take up tasks which bring benefits of money, even if we are strongly inclined otherwise. Here we have to face with courage the question of what we truly want and what we are capable of. We must also not let such conflicts make us indecisive even at the risk of making wrong decisions. Mistakes are bound to happen because our perception depends on a mind which is not always steady or clear.

Perception only happens through the instrument called mind,
which is not always steady or clear.

– Yogasūtra 2.20

Reflection

It is through the mistakes we make that we learn how to act better the next time. If we stand passively at a turning point and remain indecisive, we will be less sure of our direction, the next time we come to a crossing.

If our efforts seem to fail, we have every chance of retracing our steps, trying better the next time and learning more about ourselves. The fear of mistakes weakens our courage to rise above limitations.

Illustration: Arjuna's despair

In the epic Mahabharata we have a classic example of a warrior prince losing his decisiveness and falling into despair. Arjuna is the epitome of valour. As the foremost archer in the kingdom, he has no doubt about his ability to use his weapons in order to protect justice and the welfare of his people.

At the battlefield however, he is weighed down by hundreds of doubts. How can he fight against his own family, or aim his arrow at great people who were once his teachers, but who are all now fighting on the side of the enemy? Where is the meaning behind battles which bring a lot of bloodshed? Can justice ever be the outcome of battle? Would it not be better for him to quit the battlefield and leave the kingdom to seek spiritual enlightenment? These are questions which overwhelm Arjuna.

The intelligent answers of Krishna, his friend and teacher, also raise many questions and make Arjuna think and reflect: Does he not have to protect the welfare of people who are entirely dependent on his strength? Is it right to take a doubt so seriously when it has only arisen at the spur of the moment, when all his life he has been sure of the purpose of war? Can he, a warrior by nature, delude himself as to his true calling in order to live life as a recluse, of which he has no knowledge at all? How can he, Arjuna, decide in favour of inaction over action, when Krishna himself – teacher, god, friend, – never ceases to act? Can Arjuna's mind, which creates in him the impression that the outcome of his actions belongs to him, really bring forth a deep and meaningful query? Is it not true that finally even his very will to act is gifted to him by nature and divine forces, and does not really belong to him?

Arjuna understands that moving away from an action is not going to free him from the problems and constraints related to that action, much less lead him automatically into good action. He understands that the course of action can never be brought fully under the control of the mind, because the divine will play a role in everything. He realizes that there are greater battles to be fought. For one: to rise beyond a mind which constantly deludes him by fixing his perceptions around his own understanding and life experiences. This realisation strengthens his emotional resolve and gives clarity to his thoughts. He then enters the battle without resisting action that is corresponding with his responsibility, as well as without overestimating the value of his personal power.

Being Impatient (Pramāda)

The feeling of frustration towards oneself, or towards things one has to do, is quite common. It makes us get aggressive certain times. For example, certain tasks in daily life are a bother for us and we wish to be doing more interesting things. We find the company of some people boring and dream of people whose company could be more attractive or stimulating for us. If we are held up in a queue or a traffic jam, we want to get out of it fast enough to reach a quieter place for meditation. We are, so to say, stressed by the present situation. We will readily get aggressive in situations in which we do not really wish to be.

This absence of stillness outside merely reflects the absence of stillness within us. We begin to feel that the situation we currently are in is not good, and begin to look down on it and the people and things associated with it. We become impatient, rush through something we call unpleasant and chase what we believe to be pleasant. This makes us underestimate things, become negligent and lose our compassion. Forgetting that everything has its origin and meaning, we become haughty, proud, even arrogant.

Quelling impatience

Thinking that we can jump over a step to reach another step which we assume is more important makes us impatient and careless. It is only by strengthening compassion that we can start to give attention to the small details of life and empathize with all situations.

> *Nothing in this world is superfluous.*
> *Something that appears to be uninteresting*
> *to us now may be useful and important*
> *for another person or even to ourselves*
> *at another point in our life.*
>
> – *Yogasūtra 2.22*

In an ever-changing world, our ideas and visions need to be constantly revisited and modified according to reality. Otherwise, we become attached to our ideas and visions, or to the feelings and thoughts of the past associated with them and become restless in dealing with the present. We then have to ask ourselves whether we really have a clear idea of our vision at all. The impatience regarding an idea which has become very concrete in our minds, but not manifested in reality, very easily leads to negligence. Such negligence may even impede people who are possessed by a vision and can't wait to see it come to life.

In all these cases, learning to look at oneself from a distance can alone bring clarity and calmness. This distance to the self can only accrue from opening our eyes to the world and the people outside one's self. In short, by developing compassion.

Reflection

Negligence paired with impatience makes us incapable of looking at things calmly.

We can bring about a change in ourselves by looking at another person deeply, feeling and understanding how it is to be in his or her position. The strong emotion of compassion shines a light on the suffering happening in front of our eyes, bringing our focus to the here and now. This weakens the impatience that makes us want to move on and away from the present. Compassion reduces arrogance, calms the mind, makes us reflect quietly on the society around us and thus widens our perspective of life.

Illustration: Nārada's journey

Nārada was a great musician who had the capacity to move around singing in the heavenly regions of divine beings, thanks to his intense, unbroken devotion to Vishnu. He was aware of his unique status and had the weakness of exhibiting it too.

One day Vishnu showed him a farming couple who lived in a village and said that they were his best devotees. Vishnu saw Nārada's perplexity that these simple people lacking devotional skills could be Vishnu's favourites. He gave Nārada a bowl of milk filled to the brim and requested him to take it to his devotees, asking him not to spill even a drop.

"I met the couple. They are indeed very devout people, but they sing your praise only once a day. Otherwise, they are involved in very worldly activities", said Nārada, when he got back to Vishnu. "And how often did you think of me, when you had to carry the bowl of milk all the way to them without spilling even a drop?" asked Vishnu.

Being Indifferent (Ālasya)

Curiosity is a natural instinct in all human beings. It helps us grow, understand the world around us better and prevents us from being idle. If one is caught up in one's own self without being bothered about what is happening elsewhere, if one has no involvement in any subject other than himself or herself, curiosity as an impulse will dwindle and lead us into idleness. Idleness is a hindrance. When it overpowers us, nothing excites the mind. Idleness leads us into indifference, and in the worst case into depression.

How do we get out of this idleness and rekindle our interest? How do we regain a sense of urgency towards life and what it may bring? Indifference arises when we fail to take notice of the world around us, of its beauty or ugliness, of its joy or sorrow.

Beauty reveals itself also in its contrast to ugliness, and orderliness in its contrast to sloppiness. Curiosity will reveal to us not only the beautiful things we did not know before, but also the repulsive things we were not aware of. If we are emotionally conscious of the repulsiveness of things, we will not be able to sit back idly. It is the repulsion towards deplorable things that stops us from being indifferent. It shakes us out of idleness, and energizes us to distance ourselves so as not to get swamped by lethargy.

In life, we are confronted by many disgusting things, for example, pictures of violence, perversion and destruction. We may try to avoid confrontation with matters which we consider ugly. But the innate disgust towards them will continue to bother us. By keeping our eyes open to them and being aware of the emotion of disgust in us, we will be stirred out of our indifference and be forced to take concrete steps to move away from them. In this way, the emotional state of disgust will give us the resistance to stop consuming whatever is dumped on us, accepting whatever is told to us, or agreeing with whatever appears to be the norm.

Only through intense practice
coupled by distance to distracting things
will we reach our goals in life.

– *Yogasūtra 1.12*

Reflection

Can we afford to carry on in a superficial way and remain removed from the intensity of life? Idleness can bring us to a point where we are uninterested in discovering beautiful things and indifferent to disgusting things around us.

When beautiful things happen around you, take notice of them! When awful things happen, let emotions arise in you, and manifest in your expressions of disgust and disagreement.

Illustration: Buddha, the enlightened one

Prince Siddhartha lived a very comfortable life in the luxury of a royal palace. Within the palace walls, nobody seemed to bother about what was happening in the world outside. The prince instinctively felt that he was shut off from a big part of reality and that that would make him idle. It was his natural curiosity for the world outside that drove him to go out of the palace and see the world as it was with all its suffering. The feeling of disgust towards attachment to mortal pleasures changed his life and developed his compassion. He could never go back to the life of an idle prince and went on to become a saint. Through his love and understanding for the suffering of the world, he became Buddha, the enlightened one.

Being Distracted (Avirati)

Being constantly entertained by distracting activity can become an addiction. If we do not set a limit to entertaining distraction, these distractions will begin to set limitations to our mind. Remaining distracted will then tend to become a way of being.

Distraction leads us away from our capacity to reflect peacefully and from being in harmony with the things around us. The senses become scattered like wild horses running in different directions, who cannot pull the wagon – which is us – in one direction. The result is that we panic and get even more distracted, eventually losing our power to concentrate.

More than ever in today's world we are confronted constantly with pictures, ideas and possibilities. The media and mass communication systems swoop down on us with a never-ending barrage of commodities that we do not seek, making distraction one of the most severe hindrances in our life today. Our interests today have become so diverse that no task can really satisfy us deeply. This is a disturbing fact, for if we are occupied all the time with many things, no object will reveal itself to us in a holistic way.

The distracted or the discerning mind

We cannot resolve distractions by wiping them all out or disappearing to a remote spot where no one else exists, and then start to concentrate. It is possible to tackle distractions only by training the senses to not get carried away by the former or becoming their victim. We will need to train the senses to turn to the quiet spot within ourselves, in the recesses of our mind. To see this spot and locate oneself in it, we will need to be observant of ourselves, learn to become quiet and look calmly at ourselves.

If the senses do not get carried away
easily by external objects,
we begin to understand our inner self.
– *Yogasūtra 2.54*

In yoga, we would say that the quietening of the breath is the only way to ultimately become focussed. This can help us to taste the rasa of calmness, śānta, which is inherent in us. Instead of being distracted by things, we can remain a spectator of them. This enables us to focus our minds on objects of deep interest, self-reflection and meditation.

The skill of concentrating the mind accrues only through a deep involvement with the breath.

– Yogasūtra 2.53

Reflection

Every creative process takes time to bear fruit. It is therefore important to visualize our goal and cultivate the peace of mind to pursue it patiently. The company of peaceful beings can inspire us to visualize the state of being out of which they have drawn their energy.

Enjoying working on one thing or following up with one idea over a long period of time alone will satisfy us deeply, keep us focussed and lead us into a calm state of mind.

Illustration: The student without a master

Ekalavya's heart was set on becoming an archer and he wanted only the best teacher in the kingdom, Drona, as his master. Drona refused to accept him as a student, as etiquette prevented him from teaching a non-princely person. Drona had many disciplined students, but hardly anybody achieved mastery apart from Arjuna. One day, Drona set out into the forest with his students, to examine their skills. As each of his students exhibited his skill, the dog which had accompanied them came running out of the thickets with five arrows shot into its mouth. Arjuna removed the arrows from the dog's mouth, inspected them, assuaged the dog and looked at his teacher. Everyone was amazed, and wondered who this secret student of Drona was, who could achieve this feat! Drona himself was amazed. They all set out on a search and found Ekalavya.

Ekalavya's goal had been clear. In the past, when he had been sent away by Drona, he set out into the forest, prepared a mud-image of Drona, kept the master's inspiration constantly in his heart and practised over many years. Through his one-pointed concentration and his undisturbed reaction to having been rejected he achieved mastery as he had wished to.

Being Deluded (Bhrāntidarśana)

Those with knowledge rule over those without knowledge. Those with power decide the fate of the powerless. Man continues to colonize and manipulate others with his strong visions. This is the order of almost all social structures. Often, in the name of doing good and practicing benevolence, these structures damage the freedom and welfare of people.

How do those who wield knowledge or power know that their knowledge or power is right? They think they know better and judge what is right for others based on their convictions. The fact is that much of what we perceive is a misconception. Fooling ourselves into believing that we wield right knowledge, we pass many judgments and remain blind to truth. Keeping this delusion alive in us, we fool others too.

Once we have formed an opinion on a matter, it becomes difficult for us to admit that we have not understood it. We pretend to have a clear picture of it and are far too proud to admit that we could be mistaken. It is easier to keep the delusion alive. Having made a discovery for ourselves which we call our truth or realisation, we cling to it. As long as we do not widen our eyes or dilate our perception, we will not be able to see all sides of what we call truth.

The limitlessness of knowledge

The fact remains that truth is far too vast for us to bring into the ken of our limited perception. Knowledge is limitless, we cannot pack it into our little brains. If we raised our heads and looked high into the sky, we would realize how small we are, how limited our perception is and become open to the astonishing dimensions of truth.

Looking up, opening our senses to the immeasurable dimensions of the cosmos and of knowledge itself, can help us realize how much we do not know. Astonishment is an important emotional experience. It prevents us from settling down into our own comfortable zone of knowledge, or clinging to it. We need to appreciate, indulge and cultivate our capacity to be astonished, to fall into wonderment.

We can approach truth only step by step.

– Yogasūtra 3.6

Reflection

Truth is a vast land. If we paused for a moment and imagined its dimension, it would evoke astonishment in us. This emotion would help us keep our senses open for sensational discoveries. The moment we become too sure that we have the right knowledge, we draw boundaries around our perception and limit what we see. This makes it impossible for us to feel wonder.

Unfortunately, our thinking mind wants to rule out the impossible and misleads us into believing what we already know as correct. Wonders can happen and truth will reveal itself fully only when we drop our preconceived notions. Only then can we awaken out of this veil of illusion, look at others, listen to them without prejudice and come a bit closer to the truth.

If we reflect deeply about the mind,
we will be able to understand others fully.
– Yogasūtra 3.19

When we understand deeply the shackles
which bind us to our own selves,
we will be able to penetrate into
other beings and reside in them.
– Yogasūtra 3.38

Illustration: Śaṃkara's celibacy

We cannot have an idea of life and its phenomena without looking into them deeply and learning about them. Even Śamkara, the great scholar and unsurpassed master in the history of Indian learning had to acknowledge the limits of his knowledge. Śaṃkara travelled the entire country from the southern tip up to the Himalayas. He proved with his speeches and arguments that he was a mighty scholar who knew all the subjects regarding spiritual development. Manḍanamiśra, who was also one of the greatest scholars of the country at that time, drew him into a debate. This was judged by Bhāratidevi, the wife of Manḍanamiśra. After many days Manḍanamiśra accepted defeat and his wife took on the challenge. The debate continued for many more days. At a certain point, intimacy became the topic of discussion. Being a celibate, Śaṃkara had to reply to questions on a subject about which he did not have experience, and therefore knowledge.

Śaṃkara did not delude himself that he knew the answers. He requested his competitor for time, and left his body, after asking his students to take care of it in his absence. He entered the body of a king, who had just then passed away, and stayed in the palace leading the life of the king and learning about intimacy and the experiences that come along with it. After acquiring the knowledge, he returned to his own physical body, took up the debate from where he had left it and defeated Bhāratidevi. It was after this episode that he became respected as the highest scholar of the country.

Not Persevering (Alabdhabhūmikatva)

There are many things in life which we try and fail to achieve. For instance, we may be eating greedily and would like to eat less, but are unable to. We wish to be non-violent but keep hurting others inadvertently with criticism. The lack of success of our efforts sometimes diminishes our self-confidence, although it is actually the lack of perseverance which has caused the failure.

We often don't find the inner strength and stamina to continue working towards a goal, which we imagine is very hard to reach. This hindrance, being meek and insecure and lacking perseverance makes us think "I can't do this" or "this is not possible". Eventually we arrive at a point where we become very timid and give up tasks too early, and in that process begin to underestimate our faculties. On the one hand our mind tells us that everything is possible, but on the other, we dare less than what we are capable of.

The heavy relationship between the task and the mind

How can we muster the energy to overcome the hurdle set by our own diffident mind? What could help us make the task seem easier for our own mind?

Let us look at a mind involved with pastimes. Here amusement plays an important role and makes us treat the pastime activity as a game. We are prepared to experiment and discover our limits. We take mistakes and failures in our stride and do not blame others or ourselves. The enjoyment issuing out of such an attitude makes us want to play repeatedly and regularly and we are ready and willing to try again to attain success!

If we are too strict with ourselves, we don't have the lightness to enjoy what we do. If we carry stringent ideas about our path and its goal, failure will make us lose heart too easily.

We are amused when we become involved in our pastimes and don't get trapped in the earnestness and stringency with which we encounter our profession or relationships. The awareness of the factor of amusement helps us to retain lightness of mind, and we dare to do things which we would otherwise not.

If we realize that we are not perfect, we will be able to laugh at our own mistakes and shortcomings. Relating to the emotion of amusement and humour can help us from feeling overpowered by the objects and goals on our path. That alone will reduce our feeling of insecurity, and also lighten the seeming weight of the task before us.

To be seen is the essential purpose
of everything in the universe –
whether it is a solid object or
an abstract idea.

– *Yogasūtra 2.21*

Reflection

When we go hiking in the mountains it is the pleasure and fun we have in walking, which gives us the lightness to climb difficult stretches. If we leave the decision solely to our rational mind, we may tell ourselves that it is too difficult and give up.

We have to remember that the world is ever-changing and that life is a game, a play, a līla. It is only through humour that we can cultivate the lightness needed to perceive this way, and stop ourselves from questioning our capacity to reach the goal.

Illustration: Death Bed

Enjoyment and lightness help perseverance. A spiritual master who was on his deathbed, was surrounded by a handful of his serious disciples. They were all sad about his state and enquired after his welfare. "I never felt so good and so much in love with life," said the master, and added with a smirk, "O, I have never lied as much as now!" The anxious students urged him to give a serious answer, upon which the Master asked them to bring him a sweet. Chewing slowly, he said, "Never have I enjoyed this sweet as much as now!" and passed away.

Being Inconsistent (Anavasthitatva)

It is obvious that if we continue digging at a hole in one spot, we have better chances of finding water than if we keep shifting from place to place in a desperate search. Likewise, if we stay with one thing and follow it keenly over a long period of time, we are more likely to come to an understanding, experience or fulfilment.

There are times we have a vision and are completely sure that we can fulfil it, but change our mind and behaviour before we reach the goal and take up a new idea. We follow this new idea with great enthusiasm till the next idea comes and carries us away. Our thoughts and feelings seem to come under the influence of time, and flutter about like leaves in the wind. In spite of many of the preconditions for success, we lack the perseverance and consistency we need to reach the goal. It is as if the resolve and patience with which we started off, begin to dwindle the further we get towards our goal.

Why do we change ourselves or our tasks, without being able to stick with them continuously? Is it because things around us don't change fast enough for us that we turn away and search for something new? Is it the present-day problem of being confronted perpetually with new ideas, religions, systems of thoughts, sciences, and so on from all directions? Is it our excessive preoccupation with the results we expect from our actions? Why do we run from yoga to tennis to gym to dance to aerobics to relaxation to swimming to meditation and wind it up at the end of the week with a comprehensive medical check up to see if we are really alright? Are we victims of globalization in material and health matters, our world views, and our understanding of ourselves?

Staying with our search for a long period of time and getting closely involved with the goal might alter our way of thinking. It might lead us into spaces unknown to us. Often, it is as if an inherent fear of arriving at a climax keeps us from seeing a task through to its end. Our personal path might lead us to move home, our professional successes may bring in new responsibilities, becoming a parent can demand a change in one's lifestyle – even though all of these may be very happy circumstances, they can induce fear because they involve losses and changes. It may often feel risky to promote one's life along one's own interests, and convenient to leave things as they are. Such a fear towards matters which ideally ought not to be causing fear in us is not obvious. It is deep-seated and connected to the force which makes us hold on to life.

Fear can make us forget our resolutions and draw us away from our task. This is often so, especially when the tasks we are occupied with are not in accordance with our inner goals. If we are pursuing something because others are doing it, we are not only bound to have a weak motivation, we are also going to develop fear towards the goal that we are approaching. It is therefore important that our task and goal have a connection to our personal interest and background. If the emotion of fear is bothering us, we need to look at it, and without being cowed down, confront it.

Fear itself can be very meaningful, if it is the fear of losing sight of the larger picture. The fear of losing whatever is most precious to us can charge our actions with an urgency of purpose. Understanding fear can help us handle the unknown outcomes of our actions.

Hindrances can be overcome by
reflecting on the light within us
which never loses its glow.

– *Yogasūtra 1.36*

Reflection

Often there is a fear of getting involved, a fear of becoming too strongly linked to a purpose or a goal. It chases us into a search for new relationships, new friendships and pursuits.

But we do not find what we seek, because we don't really search deep enough.

What is it that we stand to lose? What is it that scares us? If we start to look for answers to these questions, we might rediscover what truly matters to us, what holds true meaning for us.

Illustration: The fearless women

There are many classical figures of women who, driven by strong emotions, display a tremendous amount of perseverance and limitless loyalty towards their convictions.

In Indian mythology it is Savitri's deep LOVE that helps her overcome the FEAR in following her dead husband into the nether region, to take on a debate with the Lord of Death and win back her husband's life.

It is Sita's valorous COURAGE, that allows her to enter the fire to prove her chastity and emerge unharmed because the glow of her purity is stronger than that of the fire.

It is Draupadi who, with unrelenting ANGER, keeps her five husbands motivated to fight for justice.

It is young Meera's AMAZEMENT at the vision of Krishna, that evokes poetry in her and makes her disregard all social norms to follow her vision and attain union.

In Greek mythology, Antigone risks her life to do her duty COMPASSIONATELY in conducting the death rituals for her brother, who is ostracized as an enemy of the state, and dies a sorrowful death.

Again, in the Greek mythology, it is Medea's DISGUST towards the injustices that she has to court, that she offers the life of her children to avenge the wrong done to her family.

All nine emotions work against the hindrances. They are universal: they do not belong to anyone, nor are they confined to some people only. If they heighten our ego, our efforts would become egotistic and finally crush us under their weight. For instance, a personalized dealing with emotions would mean that Draupadi's anger is only rooted in her personal feelings of revenge and is not a fight against injustice, and Antigone performed the rituals only because of her personal relationship with her brother and not because she wants to protect human values as being deeper than the rules of law and society. It would mean that Meera's love was simply carnal desire and had to do nothing with a divine calling. But it is precisely because these emotions were not exhibited or expressed in a personalized way, that they become creations of art in the form of drama, literature, poetry or thought. It is precisely because these emotions are not confined to *a* human's personal experience alone, that these tales have withstood the test of time.

What have we understood until now?

The distinction between emotions and thoughts is not a subject matter of easy or precise understanding. They all stem from our personal self, citta, as we call it in yoga. To reflect on emotions, a basic calmness and detachment of mind is necessary. If we are removed from any semblance of such a calmness or detachment, we can only wait till the intensity of the emotions have abated or take recourse to the advice of a helpful and understanding human being.

Friendliness, compassion, courage and forgiveness are intrinsic to human experience, basic traits that are embedded in us. We have to uncover them for the mind to become settled.

Nine inborn emotions have a deep-rooted permanent role in our personality. They will keep us oriented to the fundamental issues out of which the emotional disturbances are arising. Attention is required to become sensitive to the innate emotions moving within us. With attention we can recognize them and not get drawn into the myriad fleeting transitory emotions that obscure our mental clarity.

Peace of mind is obstructed often by antarāyas or hindrances which we develop. These can be overcome. Here the role of the prime emotions is very useful. Below is a list of the prime emotions and the corresponding antarāyas that they help counter:

Bhavas, our prime emotions help handle	**Antarāyas, hindrances in life**
love	illness
anger	lack of motivation
courage	indecision
compassion	impatience
disgust	idleness
calmness	distraction
astonishment	delusion
humour	insecurity
fear	inconsistency

In most philosophical systems of Indian thought, the idea of rebirth is a phenomenon that doesn't need to be proved. Similarly, the idea that we bring tendencies into the world when we are born doesn't need to be proved. These are axiomatic premises that the thought systems are further built upon.

In the next chapter we will look at deep-seated tendencies in us that cannot be removed. They are like substances out of which our minds are made. We will be speaking of these substances which remain of us after we are gone, and based upon which we are reborn.

6

KLEŚA

Five Forces Under The Surface

Kleśas are, as much as the inner instinct to survive, without a beginning.
– Yogasūtra 4.10

All Indian philosophies refer to past lives and see in the present the opportunity and the task of removing problematic tendencies and memories, called prārabdha. In yoga, the forces that work on this past, churn and bring out the tendencies and memories, are referred to as kleśas. One could say that kleśas are the essential substances which hold together and create what we call the psyche. The word kleśa comes from the root 'kls' – that which afflicts or torments. All kleśas tend to destabilize the mind. By being aware of their influence on our present, past and future actions, we gain understanding about their power and avoid becoming their target. Unlike the antarāyas, the kleśas influence very deep levels of our mind, and cannot be easily diverted or smoothened out.

Kleśas build the root,
out of which all our present and
future actions arise.
The role of the Kleśas in these actions
will be known only at a later point,
or perhaps only in the distant future.

– *Yogasūtra 2.12*

Patanjali structures the kleśas into five: one fundamental kleśa expressing itself in four forms. Being misled by illusions is avidyā, the fundamental kleśa. It expresses itself as:

Asmitā – being full of oneself, so that perception becomes self-centred,

Rāga – being attached to pleasure,

Dveṣa – being obsessed with one's hurts, and

Abhiniveśa – fearing without reason.

Pride, craving, anger and fear are very intense feelings. They all play a big role in our emotional life and cannot be tamed, or even suppressed, easily. It is only by understanding the deep space they occupy in our psyche that we can understand the influence they have on us. It is only by knowing the way they influence us that we can find a way of dealing with them and quietening their influence, so that we find our way to our prime emotions. Let us, therefore, have a closer look at each of these five kleśas.

Avidyā

Being misled by illusions, so that one becomes blind to truth

Avidyā is confusing one with the other:
the impermanent with the permanent,
the imperfect with the perfect,
the painful with the delightful and
the superficial with the intrinsic.

– *Yogasūtra 2.5*

Avidyā is the mother of the other four kleśas. Under the influence of avidyā, illusion and dreams are mistaken for reality, wrong perception for right perception. We think we know the truth when we have understood only one aspect of it.

Once we hold on to a false understanding or a falsehood, we become opinionated, and try to keep this opinion alive. We will then need to carry the burden of our opinions, which itself takes us further away from truth. In this way, the wrong perceptions within us grow in strength.

Wrong perception leads us into wrong action and from there on to results which can disrupt our balance of mind – either because we regret the results of our action or because we develop expectations related to these results. The results and our expectations related to the results let avidyā, and along with it the other four kleśas, manifest and trouble us, and eventually take hold of us fully.

Reflection

All of us would like to believe in one thing and fanatically fight for one home, one country, one religion, one idea in which we see our ultimate truth and which we call 'the right thing!' Here we have to pause and remember the role of avidyā in our understanding.

Asmitā

Being full of oneself, so that perception becomes self-centred

To mistake citta,
the fleeting self,
for draṣṭā - the permanent self
is called asmitā.

– *Yogasūtra 2.6*

The human being can not only think and/or act, but also remain a witness of their own thoughts and actions. A large part of our human self is the sum of all our actions and personal experiences, which we can relate in a biography. The most intimate and constant part of our self, however, is an aspect which has been a constant witness of this biography. We cannot describe it easily in words.

An individual human being has two aspects:

- an integral, unchanging self which is like a continuous, permanent witness that knows his or her entire life, and
- an evolving self, ever-engaged in actions or thoughts.

Both these aspects together build one's personality.

Confusing them and seeing them as one and the same is asmitā. Asmitā is that form of avidyā where we confuse the material (prakṛti or citta – the instrument that sees), with the spiritual (puruṣa or draṣṭā – the power to see). In other words, we confuse that which is fleeting with that which is permanent. The self is only a tiny aspect of the larger universal force on which it depends for existence. It has no power to stand isolated. Not seeing the interaction between the universal life forces and the self, we tend to under- or overestimate this personal self. In modern colloquial terms this self-centeredness is spoken of as 'the ego problem'.

The mind may tell us: "The world is drawing me away too much and I have to love myself and care for my needs first. Once I am taken care of, I shall develop interest for the others and the world." Such a sense of personal lack arises because we are unaware of the ever-present inner witness who accompanies all our experiences constantly. Our ignorance gives rise to the feeling that we need to attention; it makes us want to be present more for ourselves, and be more self-centred. Self-love can never lead to self-awareness. We would also have to remind ourselves that it is not the world that has drawn us away from our self but our own personal weakness and attachment that have drawn us to the world. This weakness will not go away by resorting to a self-centred attitude. The great need to attend to one's own interests is often an illusion.

Rāga

Attachment to pleasure

> *Rāga is the force which*
> *makes us expect happiness*
> *through pleasurable things.*
>
> – *Yogasūtra 2.7*

Rāga is connected to avidyā and asmitā. It is the seeking of fulfilment or happiness through an external object, person or idea. It is a longing that can never be fulfilled, because fulfilment, by its very nature, can only come from within oneself.

Greed is merely a small step away from desire. To wish for something and to desire it may be a very valid longing. But the mind leads us into believing, that the object is the carrier, the source of our fulfilment. The role of our own senses and the mind in the experience of pleasure becomes irrelevant and the object eventually rules over us. This is how Rāga becomes entrenched in us. By thinking that the pleasurable experience is linked to an object, person or idea, we lose the strength to let go of this object, person or idea and get a wrong understanding of it as well. Moreover, if the pleasurable experience is very strong, we are overwhelmed by it and cannot face the impermanence of worldly things. Eventually, we find ourselves moving away from a deep experience of happiness and peace.

Life and the human condition are impermanent. There is nothing we can hold on to, not even to a moment of bliss, much less to material goods.

Dveṣa

Being obsessed with one's hurts

Dveṣa is the force which
makes us expect unhappiness
from things we have an aversion for.

– *Yogasūtra 2.8*

Dveṣa is the opposite of rāga, and is yet another form of avidyā. We distrust objects, persons or ideas, suspecting that they will hurt us. Our judgements become based on these opinions and prejudices. This prevents us from having a neutral and equanimous understanding of what we are looking at, or who we are dealing with. Dveṣa is a force which makes us see blemishes in everything. We tend to recall moments of pain and relive them with subtle self-pity. It not only gives rise to wrong understanding of the objects, persons or ideas, but also confusion about what is real detachment, and what we really need to shun or distance ourselves from.

Reflection

During moments of frustration in a relationship, our minds will say: "I do not care for love and friendship. I have had enough of its entanglements. It does not bring me anything, and ends in fights, jealousies and passions ultimately. There is no meaning in relationships, let me move beyond all this." But it is only through a relationship with a person or an object that we can understand and empathize with it. Without a relationship, there can be only be mere seeing but no understanding.

Abhiniveśa

Fear without reason

We fear irrationally,
a fear that leads even the wise
to hold on to the impermanent.
This is called abhiniveśa.

– *Yogasūtra 2.9*

Abhiniveśa is connected to avidyā, asmitā, rāga and dveṣa. Desire and dislike for objects, ideas or persons push and pull us all the time. We cannot control or influence external objects, ideas or persons to suit our needs and visions. This makes us feel vulnerable and may make us paranoid about all kinds of real and imagined happenings, which can destabilize us or endanger our wellbeing. The limitedness of our power and possibilities is a reality. It is a fact that can worry us at any time in our life. It can also lead to a fear that is not grounded in any real object or substantial incident. This fear, abhiniveśa, shrouds our perception and leads us into illusions. It hinders us from viewing larger realities, and makes us believe that wellbeing can continue without change or an end. It makes us cling to our own selves and life, and fear death tremendously.

Fears tend to become stronger when it becomes quiet around us. At times it is like the fear of being attacked by people on a dark night when everything is quiet. We may try to overcome fears by trying to meditate and become calm. But when the mind becomes quiet in meditation, the fears may become stronger. Fear is by its nature unreasonable. It is therefore important to not give into fear meekly.

The activities of the kleśas
are not readily visible;
they must be stopped from expanding
when they are acting subtly.

– Yogasūtra 2.10

Guarding against the effects of kleśas

Kleśas are seated deep in our psyche: we can neither root them out nor suppress them. We have to deal with them intelligently. The Yogasūtra gives a clear structure that shows how the mind can be tuned to resist the influence of the kleśas. It is a structure of four steps each involving reflection, perception and action.

Through deep reflection
we can resolve the
influence of the kleśas. – *Yogasūtra 2.11*

Step 1: Heyam – realize the problem

Suffering is a part of life.

There is no way of shutting out sorrow or suffering.

One cannot minimize suffering by maximizing pleasure.

Suffering is there because you, a dependent self, are not in unison with the bigger cosmic order of which you are a part.

The realization of the nature of suffering will motivate us to work towards attaining freedom.

Step 2: Hetu – come to the cause of the problem

You can find an answer to your suffering only by looking within yourself.

Kleśas, which let loose the suffering, may be around you forever, but you need not be their victim.

Your willpower cannot undo the net which kleśas weave around you.

The kleśas are not your problems, but problems which accompany life.

Understanding the nature of kleśas will help prevent them from growing in ferocity.

Step 3: Hānam – visualize the state in which the problem is solved

Look at the world to see what beautiful mysteries it holds.

Look at the world with open eyes and astonishment to see that you are not alone in your suffering.

Deep peace, calmness of mind and happiness are states defined by the bhāvanās and bhāvas, which are inherent in us.

One can be the non-judgemental Self, observing things within and without.

There is a state of being which is truly free from sorrow. The innate yearning for freedom itself is proof that there is such a state which we can attain.

Step 4: Upāya - practice the attitudes that can solve the problem

Practice yoga in its larger context. This means making the art of yoga your way of living. It means understanding the bhāvas and bhāvanās and the basic concept of śānta rasa or vairāgya.

Whatever you do, do not forget kriya yoga, the components of which are as follows:

- put energy into your action and pay attention to it
- observe your action without being rigid and correct it if needed
- be thankful about the fulfilment derived from acting, don't ask for more
- be patient, your behaviour patterns are old and results take time

To act attentively, respecting one's own
needs and capacity without emphasizing
the benefits of the activity is kriya yoga!
Acting in this way helps
reduce the influence of the kleśas and
creates awareness for freedom.

– Yogasūtra 2.1& 2.2

Can one handle these very complex kleśas at all?

Kleśas are deep-rooted in us. We cannot get rid of them. They are beginning-less. We bring them into this life when we are born.

If these statements are true, aren't we helpless against the Kleśas?

Our system gives warnings before they begin to go out of control. By recognising the growing dominance of a kleśa in time, we can definitely work towards shielding ourselves from its onslaught. And if we have a vision of freedom that we hold, we are bound to find the strength to set ourselves free.

Avidyā, being misled by illusions, may be a basic tendency in us. But it is the event of being misled that wakes us up to seeking the truth, finding answers and resolving issues. In this way, avidyā keeps us on our toes. It plays a vital role in our life; one might even say that, in the long run, an important as well as positive one! Follies acquire meaning the moment we recognize and realize that they are follies. The follies themselves then become the motor for us to take action. From this perspective, we aren't helpless against the kleśas!

> *Avidyā is the bed on which the other kleśas thrive.*
> *The kleśas can be in different stages of intensity:*
> *dormant, tender, conspicuous or obtrusive.*
>
> *– Yogasūtra 2.4*

Like weeds in a garden, there are different grades of intensity in the way kleśas show up and influence us. They are present as seeds or roots at all times. One sees them sprout

out sometimes. This is when we can weed them out easily. When they have grown into saplings, we can still keep them under control. However, if they have become full-grown hardy weeds, we will have to put in more effort to check and control them if we want other things to thrive.

But what are we seeking? What will we be seeking? The next chapter throws light on the basic fulfilments which the human mind seeks.

7

LIBERATION

Emotions and Aims in Life

In the state of liberation
the needs of dharma, artha, kāma and mokṣa are fulfilled,
the mental balance is steady and
the inner, permanent self within
becomes clear to our perception.

– *Yogasūtra 4.34*

Fulfilment and happiness are essential life attributes that humans seek. In yoga as well as arts, we speak of three forms of fulfilment – dharma, artha, and kāma – which lead to the fourth: mokṣa.

- Dharma refers to the fulfilment related to our feeling of self-worth.
- Artha is the material fulfilment we seek.
- Kāma relates to the fulfilment we feel in relationships.
- Mokṣa is spiritual fulfilment.

1. Dharma

The word dharma in Sanskrit means holding or supporting. Dharma is the readiness to take hold of our role-based tasks and the responsibilities linked to them.

When we love someone, we take on responsibility for the emotions we create and strive to enhance the happiness of the person we love. If we are a teacher, we take on the onus of keeping our knowledge alive and valid. It becomes our dharma to be involved with deepening our knowledge. If we are a dancer, we commit ourselves to the development of our dancing skills. We follow the disciplines and responsibilities to which our activities and professions bind us. By taking interest in our actions as well as responsibility for their outcome, we also gain self-confidence.

We fulfil our dharma when we find our way to those pursuits which we feel drawn towards, and accomplish the tasks involved in those pursuits to the best of our abilities. If we fulfil our dharma, it in turn gives us fulfilment. Dharma, in this sense, leads to self-confidence and self-awareness.

How do we tune into our dharmic tasks?

To understand our dharma, it is important to reflect and do what needs to be done and not merely what we wish to do. If we are ready to answer the calls that the immediate life around us beckons with, we will be tuned to hear what our calling is. Standing up to one's tasks and responsibilities and carrying them out is the best way to gain understanding of what our dharmic tasks are. Responding to the call of dharma in this manner can reveal to us what our innate callings are and what our specific dharma is.

...that study
which is true to our nature
will bring us close to the ideals
which can guide us.

– *Yogasūtra 2.44*

How can dharma help us achieve liberation?

Acting without giving priority to the results of the action is the surest way to develop an awareness of our dharma. If we act without being propelled by benefits; if we take on the tasks life gives us without expectations; if we do whatever we can without hankering for name and fame – then, we can remain independent.

Such independence from the profits gained by an action will give us the freedom to choose those actions which truly answer the inner calling. Such actions can become liberating experiences for us.

Activities related to our professions form a large part of the activities of our life. Practicing a profession we like can help develop the attitude of taking on things which need to be done without hesitation, and without thinking of our personal interests. But even then, we have to be cautious. The course of time might lead to a change in attitude, giving room to the rise of expectations and demands.

The joy in doing an activity and the personal benefit we get from it do have a unique and unusual relationship. In doing activities that we enjoy, the thought of personal benefit does not play a conspicuous role. Conversely, whenever the idea of personal benefit dominates us, we are less bound to enjoy the activity. If we have been forced into a profession due to circumstances, and not chosen it ourselves, then personal benefit will be the predominant driver. Under such a circumstance, we will not be able to enjoy being in the profession, even if we see no way out of it. Especially then, it will be useful for us to make time to participate in activities outside the profession which fulfil us and personal benefits do not play a major role. That can slowly alter our attitude towards the profession we are in, making us feel more positive towards it. We will come see it as a way of sharing the earnings and/or knowledge acquired through our profession with others. This will give our professional activity a stronger meaning. Practising dharma in this way can become a contribution to the commonwealth.

2. Artha

The word artha here refers to material objects. Artha includes the objects we use in our daily life, our house or the land we live on, the earth and all her elements and all the bodies of the living beings on it.

Living according to the law of artha presupposes some important approaches in our relationship with objects:

- Treating them with respect, seeing divinity in them and not with a feeling of ownership. The objects have a purpose of their own and cannot be possessed by us, even if we seem to possess them in terms of legal ownership.
- When we are related to objects, especially when we claim legal ownership over them, we cannot run away from them. We have to take responsibility for and look after them.

- We cannot dump them on others or demand that others take responsibility for them.
- Even when we wish to give away material things, we do it in a way that they are looked after by someone who takes on responsibility for them.
- We cannot steal things which belong to others in responsibility.
- We do not enter into a chase to accumulate things for which we cannot take on the responsibility.

In short, we need to develop a positive relationship with the world of objects.

> *He accumulates priceless wealth,*
> *whoever refrains completely from*
> *taking away what belongs to others.*
>
> – *Yogasūtra 2.37*

How can artha help us reach liberation?

When we begin to see objects in terms of their monetary profit to us, we become greedy and our actions get entangled with the benefits. We then lose sight of the real meaning of these objects in our life. Artha then becomes something which enslaves us.

It is natural that we want to build a home and live in it. But then, a house has its own life too. If we see the house we live in as a partner who is playing a part in our fulfilment, and not a slave whom we can dispense with according to our calculations, we may develop a different attitude towards our so-called property.

Finally, nothing on this earth is really ours. We need to be happy with the opportunity we have of taking care of the beautiful things in this world and protecting them as well. We must not destroy our environment by polluting it. By protecting this world and its objects out of respect for them, we act according to the law of artha, enjoy and experience the world, and do not strive to be its master.

By stopping from accumulating things
which we do not need,
we learn who we are and
what our tasks in life are.

– *Yogasūtra 2.39*

3. Kāma

Kāma is a word with many shades of meanings and usage. It can mean rāga (desire), maitrī bhāvanā (love) or śṛṅgāra (love that includes the erotic sentiment as well). What is kāma? The word āma is usually used in the sense of erotic love, lust, desire or sexual longing. It is a powerful urge embedded in us, driving us towards uniting with a being, an object or a state. But kāma also means every form of love a human being can experience in relationships, as a partner, a friend, a child, a parent, a teacher, a student and so on.

Kāma, the sexual longing can make the kleśa of rāga grow immensely. It can create the mood of love, śṛṅgāra, with all its permanent and transitory emotions. Kāma can also be the emotional support upon which the meditative bhāvanā of maitrī, love or friendliness, can arise. In mythology Kāma is the god of Love. In the classification of the aims of life, kāma means the emotional happiness which ensues from an emotionally fulfilling relationship.

The role of sexuality

The sexual longing which attracts man to woman and woman to man, or maleness to femaleness and vice versa, is the strongest of all metaphors that symbolizes the pull of the opposites. Sexual longing motivates us to move out of our self and strive for union. This is closest in understanding the term kāma, which is a significant aspect of experiencing fulfilment. It is therefore important for us to understand sexual longing.

Sexual longing is the strongest force that can take us near the experience of moving from duality towards union. In that sense, sexuality is closely linked to the idea of happiness and fulfilment. However, it is also linked to the function of reproduction and directly connected to our instinct for survival and desire for progeny. One can therefore see in sexuality both the prospect of creating progeny as well as the prospect of attaining fulfilment and happiness.

Progeny, eternity and happiness
are to be seen in sexuality.

– Taittirīya Upaniṣat 3.10

The passage of history and societies has contributed much to confound our understanding of kāma in its aspect of sexual longing. Therefore, understanding kāma as one of the aims in life is not easy. Thanks to the damage, the relationship of societies to sexuality takes two problematic directions.

The subject of sexuality is often avoided or approached with prudishness. India has a history of understanding eroticism in the light of spirituality and in the interplay between divine and worldly happiness. However, modern values governing sexuality are modelled very much along the lines of Victorian England, which was notorious for its prudishness. According to this Victorian perspective, sexuality is seen as a means to create progeny, a carnal act and therefore impure and not leading to deep fulfilment. The role of sexuality in creating the links between happiness, union and spiritual fulfilment was shunned.

In a differently problematic approach, sexual energy is most often an expression of self-love, an instrument to subjugate, dominate or own the object of desire. This attitude towards sexuality invariably leads to aggression, whether in a subtle or obvious forms. It is very evident in the world of films. Media and advertisements misuse sexuality to instigate greed and promote consumerism. This approach can hardly be considered a tool for liberation. Such abuse or misuse of this concept keeps us continually entrapped in greedy desire. It seduces us into the illusion of being in non-duality, but actually moves us very far away from the experience of unity and oneness.

Let us therefore try to look at kāma differently. How can kāma become a step to liberation?

If sexual longing or any other form of attraction for a complementary force becomes a means to satisfy oneself only, we let rāga rule over us and there will never be an end to desire.

We need to realize that this longing and attraction can be a force which connects us to the other. Only then does it become kāma. If kāma misleads us into a self-love, it will strengthen our tendency to dominate over the other, whom we are supposedly loving. Kāma is not about being engaged and occupied with oneself but with the other. Kāma is manifest only when we open our eyes to the other, to what is outside us. If we hold the attraction for an object outside us, for a long time or stay mentally connected to it in spite of physical separation, creativity becomes possible. In this manner kāma can become the wellspring of our creativity. It will thereby also draw us away from self-love and self-centredness.

Kāma then becomes a way, not of loving oneself and wielding power over the other, but loving the other and wielding power over oneself. It will then bring us awareness about our inner strength and link us with the thought of liberation.

In India, there are many cults symbolizing divinity in sexual union. The cosmic force as sexual energy is about emotional fulfilment, and even more so about transformation to an inner experience of meditation. It would be enriching to pay attention to the knowledge of these cults, because they are embedded in an awareness from which we have moved away through the march of civilization. It would be a terrible loss, if we would ignore the knowledge of the so-called primitive tribal forms of understanding and try to pull them into the mainstream 'civilizational' culture.

Seeing in every being a part of the divine,
will give rise to immense energy.

– *Yogasūtra 2.38*

4. Mokṣa

Ideally, dharma, artha and kāma unite us with 1) ourselves, 2) the world of objects around us, and 3) the world of living beings around us, respectively. The development of these healthy relationships becomes the bedrock for moving towards a deeper goal or yearning within us, mokṣa. A deep yearning for a kind of fulfilment that cannot, perhaps, be linked to something tangible. It is the longing for a union that is not merely the deep attention and love of another person, like one's mother or partner or child. It is a yearning which binds us to a point far beyond the times when we were in our mothers' wombs. Spiritual longing, yearning for transcendence, going back to one's source, being free of every thinkable shackle – there are many forms in which mokṣa, as a need, expresses itself. However, it is always linked to a feeling of being separated and a wish to be linked and united. In this context, understanding separation and union as part of the cosmic play is important.

Keeping mokṣa in mind

Ideally, we could live in an awareness of the duality of puruṣa, the non-personal seer, and prakṛti, the citta or personal self, with the assured feeling that their union lies already in their constant attraction. Their coming together could be the sparks of creation then, the flashes of liberation.

Looking at emotions from the still foundation of śānta will help us encounter the world with vairagya, a dispassionate attitude. That will in itself be a big step towards inner freedom.

Trying to build a right attitude towards dharma, artha and kāma would automatically help us stay on the path of mokṣa.

We ought to know what our deep-seated aims in life are. That will help us to give the right place to our dreams, neither ignoring their possible relevance, nor overrating their importance, but understanding them in the context of these larger aims. This clarity can help relieve the mind of much emotional turbulence and keep it linked to the essential quest of life, namely self-awareness. Building a positive relationship with one's self, to material goods and to other human beings are in this sense definitely deep-seated aims in life.

Dance has been created and given to mankind to remove lethargy, to entertain and to teach the practitioner to stay on the path leading to fulfilment of dharma, artha, kāma and mokṣa. Thus, it was said by sage Bharata, the author of Nāṭyaśāstra:

> *There is no truth,*
> *no craft, no knowledge, no art, no yoga and no action,*
> *which is not to be found in Nāṭya.*
>
> – *Nāṭyaśāstra 1.116*

Yoga has been created and given to mankind to remove ignorance and illness which have their source within us. In fact, Patanjali is said to have given solutions to pain stemming from the body, the mind and from relationships. He is the author of *Caraka-Samhitā*, the central ayurvedic text which teaches physical health, the *Yogasūtra* which teaches mental health and the *Mahābhāṣya*, which – as a grammar book – helps correct communication.

The next chapter will go into the important subject of human relationships once more.

8

RELATIONSHIPS

Building with Boundaries

> *The entire world of tangible and abstract things can serve to entrap us as well as to liberate us.*
>
> – *Yogasūtra 2.18*

Puruṣa and prakṛti are seen as the eternal consciousness and eternal matter. They are without an origin and therefore divine. In the arts, tantric philosophies, as well as the mythological pictures, puruṣa and prakṛti are seen as Śiva and Śakti, inseparable dual powers at the source of all consciousness and creation. In yoga and in Sāṃkhya they are respectively seen as the passively witnessing and the materially evolving powers. In modern parlance we might wish to call them consciousness or ylem, prime matter. They build a duality. In the words of a poet like Kalidasa, they are like word and its meaning. They all build a duality, the absence of one precludes the presence of the other. But it is not the presence alone of both, which contributes to creativity, creation or life. It is the relationship that builds between the two, which contributes to life, as well as its evolution. Duality is the precondition for this relationship to develop. The need for this relationship is as significant to us as is our growth or vitality. Fortunately, the natural order of things forces us into this awareness of relationships.

The mind thrives on relationships. It can get agitated or quietened through relationships. From the perspectives of yoga and art and the current study of the rasas, relationships are basic to the activities of the mind. When a human relationship acquires the space it needs to thrive, not only does the relationship become peaceful, it also helps establish peace in the mind. If the space in a relationship becomes a zone of confusion, this relationship will not only run into rough weather, it will also disrupt peace in the mind.

Many emotional disturbances in life are rooted in relationships. Wherever there are confusions about the nature of relationship we have with another, we are easily led into misunderstanding. Wherever the boundaries of relationship are not clear, confusions regarding roles, misplaced expectations and disappointments abound.

Relationships may often be the field where problems manifest. However, it is through them that we learn to deal with life and the world around us. The ability to build and maintain relationships is one of the most important skills that shapes personalities. Acquiring relationship skills has a lot to do not only with being understanding about oneself and the other person, but also with knowing the space in which this relationship can flourish.

Based on sources like the Nāṭyaśāstra and the compositions of countless poets that form the choreographies, the teachers of Bharatanāṭyam trace at least nine common kinds of relationships. Each of them is based on the attitude and emotions they evoke or involve. Furthermore, each of them runs along certain boundaries, which cannot be crossed easily without risking confusion. These boundaries may appear rigid, and one may question their validity by arguing that they are mere social conventions, but clarity in relationships begins often with knowing our limits and letting them be. These are not based on morality, but on the realities of co-existence. Often it is by respecting these boundaries that it is possible to find fulfilment in dharma, artha and kāma. The nine are:

- Friend towards a friend
- Lover towards his or her beloved
- Wife towards the husband or vice versa
- Child towards his or her parents
- Parents towards their child
- Servant or employee towards her or his master or employer respectively
- Master or employer towards her or his servant or employee respectively
- Student towards the teacher
- Teacher towards the student

The idea behind this delineation of relationships is that they function in a healthy way. To become aware of the boundaries helps accept them without feeling oppressed or overpowered. We cannot find a friend in a teacher, a teacher in a lover, a mother in a master, or a wife in a servant, without courting problems. This is not a question of what is socially or ethically acceptable; there, one could have several contradictory views and positions. The delineation simply describes the reality of relationships and helps us be aware of the complications that will arise if we blur boundaries.

Clarity of relationships with other people will help us understand our roles, and cultivate knowledge of our dharma so that we can act in conformity with it. It can help us look through greed, and help us desist from things which appear green merely because they are on the other side. That can help us have a healthy attitude towards artha. It can also help us learn about love in all its shades, thereby enhancing our experience of kāma.

In a relationship between husband and wife or lover and beloved, it is the sexual longing and the surrender to each other which can inspire them to feel devotion, look beyond the individual and come closer towards the feeling of spiritual union.

In a relationship between student and teacher or between friends, the common subject of interest can bring them together to understand a larger picture of reality and therefore closer to grasping the divine.

In a relationship between master and servant, or employer and employee, it is uniting together to work on a common task that can lead to letting go of individualities and start understanding the divine.

In a relationship between parent and child, it is the idea of the magic or divinity behind life itself, which becomes the subject that unites them.

In this sense, every relationship can lead to an understanding of the divine, and therefore to a liberated state of mind.

The divine can unveil itself in myriad forms of relationships: in a friend, mother or father, teacher, lover, child, animal, flower, task. Human beings address their god as mother, father or master. They also see the divine in a child, angels, in service itself, in studies that they are dedicated to, the sound of a voice or a painting, a landscape or even the moon and the sun.

If we attune ourselves to seeing divinity everywhere, then all human relationships too will fall into place.

Eternal peace can be achieved
through surrender to the divine.

– Yogasūtra 1.23

Why do relationships play such a dominant role in life?

Relationships themselves or even the mere involvement with this theme has great value. One cannot try to do away with it. One may try to avoid the subjects of relationships and emotions, as they tend to disturb one's peace of mind easily. One may be bored by the subject and merely wish to lead a seemingly contented and simple life without complications. In such cases, one may try claim for oneself a lifestyle free of relationships.

However, relationships occupy much of our attention due to the play of emotions in them. Our emotions constantly remind us of how we relate to people, other living beings and objects. It is as if the nature of our psyche keeps us involuntarily involved with the subject of relationships, in order to push us to understand emotions. As long as relationships continue to dominate and disturb our minds, we will be drawn towards thinking about and understanding emotions. It is only through such a pull that we will move towards deep reflection on the subject and therefore feel the need to practice śānta and vairāgya –the basis of all emotions.

In other words, coming close to deep-seated experiences like śānta and vairāgya may not be possible at all without becoming involved in the subject of relationships and consequently, the emotions.

That is not all. Deep reflection and understanding of emotions will not only settle issues of relationships with others in our minds, but will also become the stepping stone towards relating well to oneself. It can become the ladder towards gaining a stable self-understanding and self-confidence. It can lead not only to peace in our relationships with others, but also to peace within the self.

Communication, relationships and emotions

Relationships develop through communication. The main wheel of communication is words, primarily the spoken word. Words spoken out loud acquire their own power, more than when we communicate these words through writing or through thoughts which are not expressed vocally.

The power of the spoken word accrues from the fact that it creates a resonance which is perceived through our ears, the subtlest of our doors to perception, from the point of view of yoga and Sāṃkhya. The word, apart from having a resonance, also denotes an object or an idea, which takes shape in our mind along with the word with which it is associated. Without the word, we would not be able to place the object or the idea in our mind. Speech, however, is not merely the verbalization of words. Apart from creating a resonance and indicating an object or an idea, feelings and thoughts accompany the words we speak and add to our communication. In yoga, one would say that it is all three – the sound, the indicated object or idea, and the feelings and thoughts (in Sanskrit, śabda, artha and pratyaya) – that together make up language.

When we speak, we are not merely conveying words, but also objects and ideas as well as emotions. Our emotions travel along with the words we express. When we speak out with certitude, we not only communicate our emotions, but also get linked to them. It is important to remember that when we speak that we are not only sharing information, but also our emotions. By communicating, we are building relationships. Language is an essential faculty of the human being.

The word, the object or the meaning it implies and
the thoughts and feelings behind them – if one
delves distinctly behind the spoken word, one can
understand the languages of all beings.
– Yogasūtra 3.17

On calmness, dispassion and fulfilment

Vairāgya is a way of coming to an understanding of the relationship our wandering mind has to our deep, spiritual self. It draws us into an intimate relationship to this Self,

the inner seer,

the inner 'eye',

the inner 'I'.

The deepest state of dispassion is linked to a
complete understanding of the Self.
– Yogasūtra 1.16

Śānta is the substratum of all emotions.

It helps us move beyond a personalized experience of emotions to

become a spectator of the drama in our own minds

– not getting drawn by them, but remaining

the inner seer who witnesses them.

Similar to the picture of the dancer who,
having created a spectacle for an audience,
recedes from it, Prakṛti, the I-substance too recedes,
when Puruṣa, the deep Self, sees its play.
– Sāṃkhyakārikā 60

Reflections

We must learn the skill of building relationships. It is the true basis for a healthy attitude towards oneself. Being dispassionately observant and calm in compassion can help us become experts in handling emotions, and thereby developing relationship skills.

Respect the boundaries along which a relationship will work: not to conform to morally, socially or politically correct norms, but to be in tune with the reality of the context and the persons involved.

Puruṣa and prakṛti can be seen as the ideal for all relationships. Duality, which is the pre-condition of a relationship, is definitely important and real, but oneness is as real and inevitable! This is the subject of the concluding thoughts in the following chapter.

9

AṢṬANĀYIKĀ

The Eight States of a Loving Mind

Yoga philosophy speaks of a skilful relationship to the outside of the self as the initial step. Only as step two will we be capable of relating to oneself, to that which is within. One of the definitions of yoga is 'relationship', meaning the togetherness of puruṣa and prakṛti, also seen as Jīvātmā and Paramātmā, or the deep personal Self and the non-personal part of us, where we are connected with the eternal cosmos. In other words, when the citta is in a perfect relationship with the draṣṭā, life flows in a harmonious way.

Love in all its different states is the essence and driving energy in this relationship which Nāṭya talks of and which yoga aims at: the relationship between the human and the divine. Like every other relationship, it is wrought with emotions - sometimes fearful, sometimes full of love and longing. A sense of awe and being far away from the divine may dominate, leaving us with a feeling of being lost in a hierarchy, but it is intimate all the same.

Nāṭyaśāstra portrays this relationship as the Nāyikā-Nāyaka-Bhāva. This is the central theme of Nāṭya. Here the dancer acts as a female in love, called Nāyikā, literally the woman who is leading or showing the way, a representation of the human soul. The object of her desire is the Nāyaka, seen as a man or eternal soul. The onlooker watches the Nāyikā talking to the beloved of her imagination: here love is the sthāyi bhāva. It is similar to a public prayer but full of erotic charge. Through nāṭya, dance, the Nāyikā leads the onlooker to the divine. According to ancient Indian traditions, the arts are a symbol of the relationship between the human and the divine. Here, as in yoga, the lover is seen as Prakṛti (matter) and the beloved as Puruṣa (consciousness).

The eight Nāyikās or eight heroines are synonymous with the different states in which the mind in love can be. The onlooker can empathize with the different situations: being separated from or reunited with the beloved, or waiting and yearning for the beloved in life. But now the onlooker can transcend the yearning into a divine relationship between her or his own and the eternal soul. The Nāyikā leads the onlooker through poetry and dance to the desire for the divine, to that point which is infinite love. Representing the moods of the onlooker, the dancer as a Nāyikā is a woman separated from the beloved, awaiting or scolding the beloved – in a deep dialogue with her chosen god (the divine).

Sometimes the Nāyikā is portrayed as talking to her imagined friend, the sakhī (literally, a female friend), about her love for this absent god. She expresses her yearnings and thereby acts out what everyone in the audience may feel: I am separated from the truth, I am not in samadhi, I am not spiritually enlightened, even if I long for it. I am still seeking.

It is only by constant awareness of the difference between the impermanent mind and the eternal, undisturbed 'Seer' within us, that we become masters of all emotions and all knowledge.

– *Yogasūtra 3.49*

An understanding of these eight nāyikās helps us to see divinity in all relationships.

Guru and Bhakti

In the context of the eight nāyikās, the sakhī is an important figure in poetry, dance and drama. The sakhī is the female companion, who also acts as a messenger between the lover and her beloved. She knows the way to the beloved. The beloved being, in this case, the divine itself, the sakhī acquires the significance of not only a friend, but also a guru, a teacher in a spiritual context.

It is not easy to talk directly to one's beloved when deeply in love. All complaints, sorrows and whispers of secret love, the letters and the ecstatic happiness of the loving heroine are addressed by the nāyikā through her various dances to the sakhī of her imagination. The sakhī listens and becomes an advisor as well as messenger. Some dances, however, portray the sakhī herself, who speaks as a guru to the nāyikā. The nāyikā finds in the sakhī a trustworthy friend who lends her ear and gives guidance, but most of all enables her, the nāyikā, to shed all her inhibitions, overcome all her apprehensions and express her intense love for the divine.

Bhakti is the love for the ultimate divine, which is indestructible and all-encompassing. Bhakti is an emotional feeling which stems from our longing to be linked to the divine. The human mind senses a need for permanence and wishes to connect its feelings and thoughts with that permanence.

> *Through constant surrender the deepest self in us becomes evident, while antarāyas diminish.*
>
> *– Yogasūtra 1.29*

A nāyikā is the soul which is seeking union. In the context of bhakti, all human beings are seen as feminine nāyikās in search of transcendence. Each facet or state of love reflects an inner awareness. Therefore, a nāyikā can be acted out on stage by a male, female or transgender dancer portraying femininity as the quality of surrendering.

> *Through deep meditative reflection on one subject, knowledge of all subjects can be attained.*
>
> *– Yogasūtra 3.5*

The eight states of the loving mind are:

Svādinapattikā – being fulfilled
The lover is in a state of oneness with the beloved.
Vāsakasajjakā – awaiting
The lover prepares for the arrival of the beloved.
Virahotkaṇṭhitā – longing
The lover pines for the beloved.
Vipralabdhā – lamenting
The lover despairs and starts to give up hope.
Khaṇḍitā – being agitated
The lover dismisses the beloved, doubting his sincerity.

Kalahāntaritā – regretting

The lover is stirred into awareness for the beloved.

Abhisārikā – loving fearlessly

The lover follows the beloved fearlessly.

Proṣitabhartṛkā – accepting separation

The lover trusts the beloved who is on a mission in a faraway place.

These eight states are a poetical theme in almost all the love songs in Indian art. In many popular love songs, the beloved is Krishna. Rādhā, his female counterpart symbolizes the loving, human soul. The dancer as nāyikā is Radha and portrays the different states of the human mind through different love songs. The audience can reflect on them. The performance becomes a meditation on Krishna and Radha, Puruṣa and Prakṛti.

The following brief portrayal of each state of the different nāyikās is embellished by the following:

- a phrase from poems which are part of the repertoire of Indian dance,
- a sutra from the Yogasūtra,
- the landscape enhancing the mood based on the descriptions in Tolkāppiam, an ancient Tamil text on art and literature
- a modern poem.

Each state is a call to appreciate the beauty of emotions.

To meditate on love will give rise to infinite love.
– Yogasūtra 3.23

Svādinapattikā: The fulfilled nāyikā

In ancient Tamil literature, in Tolkāppiam the landscapes were associated each with an emotion and inspired poetry.

The mountains are the landscape for union (Tolkāppiam-*kurinji*)

Bliss in union

Rādhā and Krishna are together and happy. Gladdened by her beauty and grace, Krishna stays by Rādhā's side and praises her. She reclines in his divine form; her love is free of doubt. Rādhā enjoys the full moon and the sandalwood paste that Krishna puts on her breasts. The natural world around them is in a state of peace. Rādhā, the human soul, has become a goddess for Krishna, the god. He is at her feet.

> *"O Krishna, put the silver belt with the jewels back on my hips to cover my nakedness..."*
>
> *– Gītagovindam, Act 12, Verse 21,)*

Union in yoga is the aim and fulfilment of meditation.

> *In the pure state of enlightenment, the mind is still, no activities of thought or memory cast a shadow on the purity of this state.*
>
> *– Yogasūtra 1.43*

Vāsakasajjakā: The awaiting nāyikā

The forests are the landscape for the awaiting. (Tolkāppiam-*mullai*)

In a-waiting bliss

Krishna waits for Rādhā. He decorates the bed with flowers. He is happy when he thinks of his beloved and prepares himself for the imminent union. Everything he does is filled with the knowledge of her arrival. He knows, and is sure, that she is coming. All his thoughts and feelings are directed only on Rādhā's arrival.

> *"O Radha! Hearing the slightest sound – a bird landing on a tree, a fluttering leaf – He imagines you have come. He joyfully prepares the flower bed, and anxiously watches the path for Your arrival."*
> *– Gītagovindam, Act 5, Verse 10*

Even the divine has its need to be united with the mundane. The feminine aspect of Krishna finds its expression here. The sakhī describes Krishna's longing for Rādhā.

A deep state of meditation emerges when feelings and thoughts unite to focus on a theme that can elevate. Here, impatience may still be there, but also deep trust that the meditative state of inner quiet, where all other things do not matter, can be found.

> *In the state of dhārana the mind is spellbound to one single object of devoted attention.*
> *– Yogasūtra 3.1*

Virahotkaṇṭhitā: The longing nāyikā

The beaches are the landscape for pining (Tolkāppiam-*neithal*).

In separation from bliss

The moon has arisen, Krishna has not arrived. Rādhā begins to feel the pain of separation and is dreadfully unhappy. She does not eat or drink, falls on her bed without being able to sleep, continues to think only about Krishna. She fears that he is with another woman and does not love her anymore. Everything that is beautiful reminds her of her love and she suffers.

> *"O Krishna, the cool rays of the moon are scorching Rādhā, the soothing mountain breeze feels to her like the hissing of a viper... the thoughts of you make her faint - and yet she only thinks of you..."*
>
> – *Gītagovindam, Act 4, Verses 2-8*

The human mind is most of the time in a state of separation and longing – longing for the beloved one, an object or an aim. Longing keeps the mind connected to the object of love and can thereby help focus it. But it can also bring about fear of losing the object of love, agitate the mind and become a hurdle for meditation.

> *If the meditative state is disturbed, all disturbing inclinations of the mind become active.*
>
> – *Yogasūtra 4.27*

Khaṇḍitā: The agitated nāyikā

The towns, villages and fields are the landscape for quarrel (Tolkāppiam-*marutam*)

In the absence of bliss

The agitated nāyikā has been waiting the whole night for Krishna. She is lovesick, her heart wrenched by jealousy. Her torment expresses itself in angry bursts. When Krishna arrives in the early hours of the morning, she scolds him and sends him away, although she loves him dearly.

> *"Oh Krishna, was the moonlight so bright, that you confused my house with hers? That fish-eyed beauty has left marks of kisses on your lips. Has she not satisfied your longing? Why have you come here into my street? Go, go away, I am not that girl."*
> *– Padam composition in the Tamil oral tradition*

The scolding nāyikā is a symbol of one's ego standing in the way of bliss. Out of foolishness, one sends away what one desires, and is bound to suffer and regret it later. On the spiritual path, one needs to become aware that the object of love cannot be possessed: the divine belongs to all.

> *By meditating on the bonds which tie our mind and loosening them, we can become capable of slipping into the mind of others.*
> *– Yogasūtra 3.43*

Vipralabdhā: The lamenting nāyikā

The deserts are the landscape for separation and lamenting (Tolkāppiam - *pālai*)

Lamenting over the absence of bliss

The nāyikā complains about her state of separation, she sighs and weeps. She removes her jewels and throws open her hair. She is in despair and finds no comfort in anything.

But even as she despairs and complains, she knows that she continues to love Krishna, as he is verily the divine.

> *"O my sakhī, He is for ever unfaithful. It is an utter waste of my feelings, yet when I think of Him, my heart becomes wild with love...!"*
> *– Padam composition of Kshetrayya in Telugu*

When we connect our personal suffering with awareness for a cosmic order, we can gain a meditative experience. In this way, all suffering can be a way to hope and belief. It can become a strength to prepare us for deep prayers. Weeping and lamenting makes us seek a higher force which is the source of all things. Like a child weeping and calling out for its mother, similarly the adult too searches for a divine power to gain strength. All this can happen only when we look at our suffering and express it.

> *By meditating intensely on the heart, we attain a complete understanding of our self.*
> *– Yogasūtra 3.24*

Kalahāntaritā: The regretful nāyikā

Regretting the separation from bliss

Rādhā regrets that she has scolded Krishna, yet she sighs and complains about him. Being troubled by her feelings, she admits to herself that she loves him and hopes inwardly that he will return to her.

> *Sakhī to Rādhā: "Do not be angry with Krishna. The passion in your ripe breasts! Should it be wasted? My dear, do not let your heart be lonely!"*

– Gītagovindam 9.2

Meditation can start only when the burden of the ego on the mind is lightened. Only then can feelings reveal their non-personal power. Realisation that comes through regret helps us leave behind our self-centred outlook. When we realize that our expectations have been too high, we understand why our disappointment is heavy. When we realize that our reaction was out of balance, we can see through the shallowness of the games the mind wants to play and its lack of reliability.

Reflection on how the senses get involved with
things makes the mind stable.

– Yogasūtra 1.35

Abhisārikā: The fearless nāyikā

The fearless nāyikā walks through all landscapes.

Fearlessly following the path to bliss

The nāyikā gives up all doubtful thoughts and develops great strength. She walks through the forests to meet her lover and feels no fear at all; nor does she bother about how she is clad or about the gossip of the neighbours. She braves every obstacle and pitfall, with the relentless thought of uniting with the divine.

Let's go,
where the tribes wear
the narcotic wreaths of cannabis
beyond the land of katti,
the chieftain with many spears,

let's go, I say, to where my man is,
enduring even
alien languages.
(Ancient Tamil Poetry, Māmụlanār, Kur 11)

True love makes fear disappear and paves the way for unconditional surrender. The connection to a oneness is unhindered and there is no confusion of emotions. When the inner voice leads, boundaries are no more hindrances. Beauty and strength radiate from a person in a fearless state.

If our meditation is like that and we are totally one with the theme of our meditation we have reached a high state of dhyānam. Self-centred thoughts no longer distract us from within. Here our prayers are full of emotional fervour and we are sure that they will be heard.

If draṣṭā, the permanent Self within us guides all our deeds, we lose the desire for personal achievement.

– Yogasūtra 4.25

Proṣitabhartṛkā: The lovelorn nāyikā

The landscape for loss and separation is in the deserts (Tolkāppiam – *pālai*)

Unending separation and loss of bliss

The nāyikā remains strong in her faith in him. Her beloved is out of reach. She accepts that happiness and bliss, like life itself, are unsure.

People say, "You'll have to bear it". Don't they

know what passion is like, or is it that they are so strong?
As for me, if I do not see my lover
grief drowns my heart,
and like a streak of foaming high waters
dashed on the rocks
little by little I ebb
and become nothing.
(Ancient Tamil Poetry, Kalporu Cirunuraiyar, Kur 290)

At times, the object of our love is out of reach due to circumstances. Or we have to accept its loss. By accepting the reality as it is and yet remaining full of trust and strength that nothing in this universe gets lost and souls unite again, we gain great strength. We might be far away from the enlightened state, but we can remain faithful to the aim. Without developing fear, the mind can arrive in deep calm. We will need to surrender all thoughts of profit from our efforts and interests. Only then do we have a strong basis for meditation. Surrendering without meekness, accepting without feeling humbled, being separated and yet connected: the state of love portrayed by this nāyikā is indeed very deep.

By staying linked to the source of light within us,
we become capable of discerning things which are
subtle, very far away or unrecognizable.

–Yogasūtra 3.25

10

PEACE AND PASSION

Union in Separateness

The concept of puruṣa and prakṛti is central to Indian philosophy. They represent depending on the context the divine and the mundane or the mundane and the divine, consciousness and matter, the immovable and the movable. They are dual powers which guide us also from within and reflect the duality which we face in life. We have the female and the male side to each of us. By accepting this and engaging ourselves with it, we can become aware of the unity which abides behind all dualities. Looking at and through this duality can help lead us to the inseparable unity that lies behind it.

There is great beauty and freshness in each leaf of a tree in spring, they shrivel and become brown and brittle in winter before they are gone, to once more return the next spring. And if the tree collapses of old age, it leaves back seeds that build new trees. Life and death build a circle and there is divinity in this unperishable oneness. It is the same with Love. It is there, when we are furious and angry. It is a wise outlook to see the union of things and emotions and not merely that which separates them. Dance celebrates this and inspires us, by creating a greater awareness of all the senses and their scattered existence, without leaving us judgemental and disappointed. Yoga celebrates this by teaching us to be aware, alert and compassionate at all times and remain conscious of the unity behind all dualities.

In no Indian temple of olden days do we find a Rama abiding without Sita to his side. A sheer male symbol is a show of patriarchy contrary to the concept of the oneness of the forces within and without. War too loses its meaning if it is taken out of the context of peace. Almost no war of today's world is established in this context, but made to win land or feel pride and victory. Passion is not directed to peaceful existence but towards gaining and winning. Such utter separation in thinking of good and bad, divine and evil is the great sickness of our times.

If dancers are seducers, we need to question what they are seducing us into. The answer is: To a higher state of awareness. If Yogis are ascetics, we need to ask what they are aiming at. Here too the answer is: to a higher state of awareness. Seduction and austerity are also one.

Duality need never be at the exclusion of unity. In fact, it is the presence of duality which makes us aware of unity, prods us on to unite different views, tolerate thoughts which are contrary to ours and understand that they all belong to the great unity of existence. By acknowledging the within and the without, the internal and the external - the personal self and the cosmic Self -, we can begin to bridge the gap between them. We can let go of our attachment to ourselves, face the unknown across us without fear and include what we cannot understand or what remain strange to us, also as a part of our knowledge.

The goal in art is to bring together the opposites, things which are so far apart that they seem to be incompatible, like the divine and the mundane. In this sense it is a yogic meditation, where the Seer and the Seen come together.

This is what deep reflection is for: it is the beginning of a meditative state.

> *In the deepest state of meditation, samādhi, the observed subject alone glows; it is, as if the observer has resolved into it.*
>
> – *Yogasūtra 3.3*

Despite the strong images of a masculine Śiva and a feminine Śakti, both puruṣa and prakṛti are part of each human being, irrespective of her or his gender. When we stay linked with this divine image – represented as the couple, Puruṣa and Prakṛti – the desire to be seen as a woman or man diminishes. Not only do false identifications based on the idea of being 'male' or 'female' become less relevant. Every identity – of nation, language, gender, faith or status – appears like a veil which merely separates oneself from others. In the light of a comprehensive understanding of one's self as the partnership of Puruṣa and Prakṛti, this veil loses its significance. We overcome barriers and move towards emotional liberation.

Ultimately suppressing emotions will always have negative results. Anger is inspired by the sight of injustice, love by the feeling of separation, disgust by the need to distance ourselves from undesirable things, courage by the drive to achieve what is above the ordinary; amusement enables us to look at things from different perspectives, compassion goads us into understanding suffering, fear makes us aware of the limitations of our resources and astonishment opens our eyes to the larger order of life. If you oppress anger, you lose your sense of justice. If you oppress compassion, you become incapable of handling suffering. If you oppress love you become lonely. If you oppress the natural feeling of disgust, you lose your resilience towards undesirable things. If you oppress fear, you become ignorant.

Try to find your way to the emotions. Find an object of your love. Enjoy your love for this object. Do not try to possess it. Enjoy its existence outside of you. It is the opposite force. Try to become the witness of your own mind and its movements.

Thus, Nāṭyayoga begins.

BIBLIOGRAPHY

Natyasastra, Adya Rangacharya (transl.), IBH Prakashana, Bangalore, 1986

Nāṭyaśāstra of Bharatamuni, K. Krishnamoorthy (ed.), Oriental Institute, Vadodara, 1992

A Dancer on Dance, V.P. Dhananjayan, Bharata Kalanjali, 1984

Abhinayadarpanam, Edited & translated by Dr. M. Ghosh (transl and ed.), Manisha Granthalaya, Calcutta, 1975

Way to Liberation: Mokṣa Mārga, Alamelu Sheshadri and T.K. Sribhashyam, D.K. Printworld, New Delhi, 2011

Religiousness in Yoga, T.K.V. Desikachar, Skelton and Carter (eds.) Lanham: University Press of America, 1980

Patanjali's Yogasūtra, T.K.V. Desikachar, Affiliated East-West Press, New Delhi, 1987

The Heart of Yoga, T.K.V. Desikachar, Inner Traditions, Vermont, 1995

Yogasūtra, Transliteration, Translation and Paraphrase, R. Sriram, unpublished manuscript.

Descartes' Error: Emotion, Reason and the Human Brain, Antonio Damasio, Penguin Books, New York, 1996

Gitagovinda of Jayadeva, Narayana Gosvami Maharaja (transl.), Gaudiya Vedanta Publications, 2005

The Interior Landscape, Clasical Tamil Anthology, Translated by A.K. Ramanujam, Clarion Books, Delhi / London